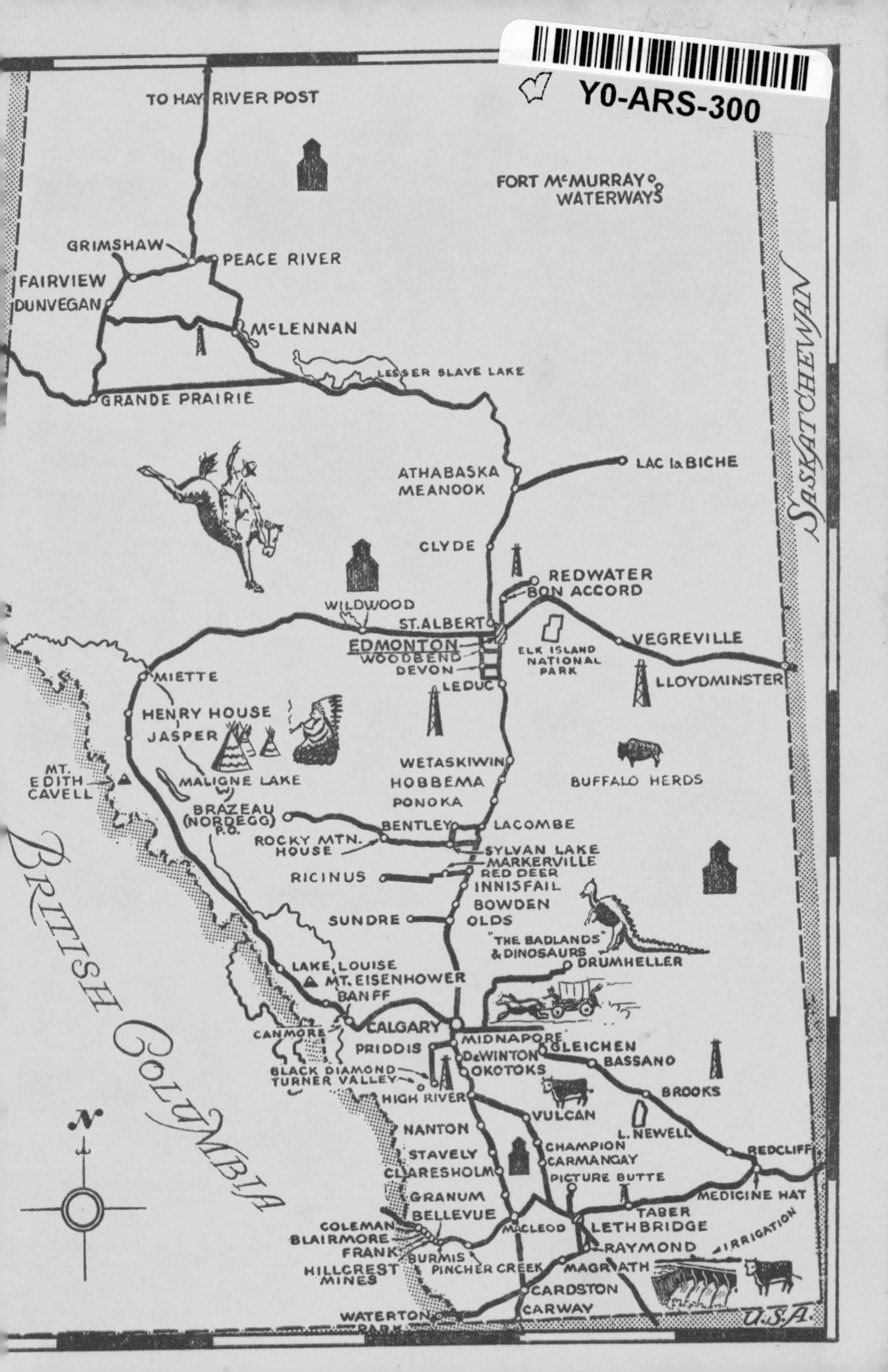
TO HAY RIVER POST
FORT McMURRAY
WATERWAYS
GRIMSHAW
PEACE RIVER
FAIRVIEW
DUNVEGAN
McLENNAN
LESSER SLAVE LAKE
GRANDE PRAIRIE
SASKATCHEWAN
ATHABASKA
MEANOOK
LAC la BICHE
CLYDE
REDWATER
BON ACCORD
WILDWOOD
ST. ALBERT
EDMONTON
WOODBEND
DEVON
ELK ISLAND NATIONAL PARK
VEGREVILLE
LLOYDMINSTER
LEDUC
MIETTE
HENRY HOUSE
JASPER
MT. EDITH CAVELL
MALIGNE LAKE
WETASKIWIN
HOBBEMA
PONOKA
BUFFALO HERDS
BRAZEAU (NORDEGG) P.O.
BENTLEY
LACOMBE
ROCKY MTN. HOUSE
SYLVAN LAKE
MARKERVILLE
RED DEER
INNISFAIL
RICINUS
BOWDEN
OLDS
SUNDRE
BRITISH COLUMBIA
"THE BADLANDS" & DINOSAURS
DRUMHELLER
LAKE LOUISE
MT. EISENHOWER
BANFF
CANMORE
CALGARY
MIDNAPORE
PRIDDIS
GLEICHEN
DeWINTON
BASSANO
OKOTOKS
BLACK DIAMOND
TURNER VALLEY
HIGH RIVER
BROOKS
VULCAN
N
NANTON
L. NEWELL
CHAMPION
CARMANGAY
STAVELY
REDCLIFF
CLARESHOLM
PICTURE BUTTE
GRANUM
MEDICINE HAT
BELLEVUE
TABER
COLEMAN
LETHBRIDGE
MACLEOD
IRRIGATION
BLAIRMORE
RAYMOND
FRANK
BURMIS
PINCHER CREEK
MAGRATH
HILLCREST MINES
CARDSTON
CARWAY
WATERTON PARK
U.S.A.

THIS IS ALBERTA

THE RYERSON TRAVEL LIBRARY

THIS IS NOVA SCOTIA, *Will R. Bird.*

OVER ON THE ISLAND, *Helen Champion.*

THIS IS ONTARIO, *Katherine Hale.*

THIS IS NEW BRUNSWICK, *Jessie I. Lawson and Jean M. Sweet.*

'ROUND NEW BRUNSWICK ROADS, *Lilian Maxwell.*

MANITOBA ROUNDABOUT, *Lyn Harrington.*

THE LURE OF MONTREAL, *W. P. Percival.*

THE LURE OF QUEBEC, *W. P. Percival.*

THIS IS ALBERTA

KEN. E. LIDDELL

THE RYERSON PRESS ~ TORONTO

Published May, 1952
Reprinted October, 1953

ACKNOWLEDGMENT

To those many friendly people who took time from their work to tell me of themselves and their communities, and to *The Calgary Herald* for permission to use material that was gathered for that paper: Thank you.

PRINTED AND BOUND IN CANADA
BY THE RYERSON PRESS, TORONTO

THIS BOOK is respectfully dedicated to the spirit of the people who have developed Alberta and to those who are continuing the job.

And when should one visit Alberta to see what has been done and is being done amid its peaks and on its plains?

Oh, drop in any time and just as you are for "the latch string is always out."

Contents

List of Illustrations

1

Smile of the Princess

THERE is something about Alberta that is written in the sky. It is not the legendary pie in the sky, for Alberta does not reach for its riches. It has them at every turn in oil, natural gas, coal, minerals, agricultural and range produce, forest resources and the great playgrounds of nature that are the Canadian Rockies, so silent, so beautiful and in their old age worth millions in tourist traffic.

What Alberta has in the way of a sky is substantially the same as what covers the rest of the world, but in the great reaches of the west it can happily stretch itself from horizon to horizon and in Alberta it has a sunny smile of contentment for a land that is so young, so beautiful and so wealthy it is aptly known as the Princess Province.

To the visitor, Alberta's sky is as much of an attraction as its great mountains. Its sweeping beauty is shown on the crest of the Province. Chosen in 1907, the crest depicts a blue sky above a range of snow mountains, a range of green hills and a wheat field surmounted by a prairie. At top of the crest appears the St. George's Cross on a white background.

Under that sky and within the protection of that crest live people who come from all races but who now share a family tree that has stout-hearted roots in the courage of the explorers, police, traders and missionaries and its heritage in the great open-heartedness of the west.

Alberta has been referred to lately as the Texas of Canada. It is a reference due chiefly to its bountiful seas of oil. But it is more than that. An Albertan is as proud of his Province as a Texan is of his state because, although he is more modest about it, he firmly believes his Province has the biggest this and the biggest that and is the greatest in Canada.

He believes this with pardonable pride. He knows Alberta has some of the greatest scenery in the world. Its oil development since 1947 has made the Prairie Provinces self-sufficient in petroleum and the Albertan sees no reason why his Province should not make all of Canada self-sufficient in the same need in another five years.

Alberta has the greatest irrigation in the land and while fishing is good all over, one of those very irrigation dams, at Bassano, as far back as 1913 produced a veritable giant of a sturgeon weighing 78 pounds, measuring three inches over six feet. Today it is well preserved in the beverage room of the Imperial Hotel at Bassano, and those who recount its history never fail to mention the fact that the chap who caught it was fined for illegal fishing.

On a cold day Albertans wax warmly over the fact their Province has enough coal to last all Canada for 1,200 years at the present rate of consumption.

To speak of Alberta's beef with anything but respect is treason. Every summer hundreds of thousands jam Calgary for a prairie mardi gras known as the Calgary Stampede which is also a tribute to those who roam the range. Albertans would probably call it the greatest show on earth but some circus fellow thought of that first so they settle for the greatest outdoor show of its kind on the continent. To them it is no circus, but a tradition.

Alberta's agricultural resources range from great fields of waving wheat on dry land to sugar beets that in the fall harvest are piled almost as high as the sugar factories themselves in the irrigated areas. Alberta knows that what is grown on the land, coupled with what is grazed from it, is still its very foundation and each year it honours what it calls its Master Farm Families. To them go substantial cash awards, a gift of their government—and so from the people themselves—and a plaque to hang on the farm gate which, for all of the progress one finds just as difficult to open in Alberta as anywhere else in the west, and harder to close once one has it opened.

Alberta's natural gas is in itself something worth blowing about. Utility consumption throughout the Province in 1950 was 51.5 billion cubic feet and estimated reserves totalled 4,400 billion cubic feet. These were eyed with envy by other Provinces and even states of the union which were wooing Alberta with offers of pipelines to export the gas from the Province that itself was dangling such cheap fuel before industrialists to successfully start itself on the road to becoming an industrial empire.

It would not take a man long to lose himself in the forests that have 30 billion cubic feet of saw material, or in the great expanse of the north country where resources are barely tapped.

That is why Alberta's future is as bright as its skies are sunny as they beckon the highway traveller who is often startled by such signs as a huge thumb that points high and urges: "Look up. The cleanest sky in the world is above you."

Richly endowed by nature, Alberta's greatest heritage, however, is in her people. The Province has many things to draw others to it, but it is the neighbourliness of the people that makes them want to stay.

It is a neighbourliness that probably is best described by an experience of W. P. Rawles, one of the hundreds of geologists who these days roam the back roads of the Province.

Mr. Rawles was driving in the vicinity of Morningside, somewhere halfway between Calgary and Edmonton, when he was hailed by a farmer. The farmer asked Rawles if he would tell so and so up the road that his cow was sick in this chap's pasture. It was a bit out of the way, so Rawles was given directions. When he came to what he thought was the farm, Rawles drove in and delivered the message to a man who met him in the yard.

The farmer pondered for a moment, said it was not his

cow that was sick but he would go over and look after it because he knew whose cow it was.

"He is my neighbour," the man explained.

In four simple but dignified words the farmer epitomized the neighbourliness of the West and particularly of Alberta.

This, then, is not offered as a history of Alberta. There is some history in it, but only for background. What you are starting is a wandering and may it be a happy visit among people I am proud to say are my neighbours, and as you get to know them may you also appreciate the wealth of character that is in the make-up of any person you may meet who says: "I am an Albertan."

2

The Macleod Trail

WHEN you travel south of Calgary on the black-topped No. 2 highway toward the American border, you are travelling along an old stage coach road that today is known as the Macleod Trail. But this is a misnomer, for should you start from Macleod, one hundred miles south of the foothills city, to go northward to Calgary, you'd be on the Calgary trail. What you call it depends upon which way you are going, and it has the same difference in another respect.

The rolling country from Calgary southward to High River, about forty miles, is the most beautiful of its kind you'll find anywhere. The majestic mountains rise to the west. They are some forty miles distant from the highway, but atmospheric conditions at times make them appear to be a stone's throw away.

To the east, the flat prairie stretches endlessly to eventually meet with the sky and to make the traveller of today feel that those hardy souls who ventured westward from old Fort Garry, or the western gateway at Winnipeg, in their creaking Red River carts not only endured a rough but also a most monotonous trip.

But this particular forty miles between Calgary and High River is enough to catch the breath of any lover of nature's beauty. And if he is at all observant, and lucky enough to travel both ways between the two points, he'll notice a peculiarity of the country.

It is the same country no matter which way he is covering it, but it develops a different viewpoint.

A hardware store clerk in High River once told me he'd made a 3,000-mile vacation trip by auto through the northern United States, back through the Canadian Rockies to Banff thence to Calgary and back home. He said he'd never seen such beautiful country as there is between High River and Calgary, which he'd covered many times.

He pointed out that it is more beautiful going between High River and Calgary, or northward, than it is the other way. Try it some time. It's a fact. The sweep of valley as you approach Calgary, the country ahead that seems to roll like an endless roller coaster, is something never to be forgotten.

But then it is really nothing unusual for Alberta's scenery to change its stripes. When you are out in the mountains, what you see varies by the hour with the changing light.

We are on the Macleod Trail and going south. Travelling over a historic trail that today is a smooth, modern highway so much used by the oil and tourist traffic and the neighbours coming and going that it has been forced to stick out its shoulders into a four-lane highway for the first fourteen miles to Midnapore.

Midnapore used to be Fish Creek and it is the first place you drop into after leaving Calgary. You also drop into an interesting story of how it became Midnapore, a name probably more refined if less picturesque than Fish Creek, although the water that trickles its way through the community is still doing business under the old name.

It is at Midnapore that you find two of the most quaint churches in the country. They sit, side-by-side, on the east side of the road. One is Anglican, the other Roman Catholic. The Anglican church has such quaint architecture that it appears to have been built for a congregation of thin people.

All this area was once the domain of the cattle king, the late Senator Pat Burns—for whom the trees bordering the road are a memorial, although that is another story—and a yarn the folks never tire of telling is how Senator Burns would send a crew down to paint the Catholic church and tell them to paint the Anglican church, too, because he liked things spick-and-span.

The man who told me of this was Hugh Shaw, and it was he who recalled the strange story of how Fish Creek became Midnapore.

In Hugh Shaw I was talking with a big man who wore a big hat and smoked a big pipe and who looked back on life with a sense of humour. An expansive man like the country in which he was raised.

He remembered the time his father had an argument with the Calgary council over tax concessions. The father had wanted to set up a woollen mill in Calgary in the days when people were less concerned with taxes on their land than they were in getting there first to sit on it the longest so they could get it for nothing. There were many hardships for those early settlers, but in some respects development of the western country was a dead give away. But they had fun.

Shaw remembered the time he and another friendly wag tied a stuffed goat over the pulpit of one of the churches down his way and just when the minister was about to blast the devil, the goat came down on his noggin. The minister went ahead blasting the devil then turned his attention to some of the devil's young friends, and so spoiled the joke.

Shaw could also remember the days when the trains would stop to give the settlers' creaking wagon caravans a supply of water. He remembered the Riel Rebellion chiefly because he (Shaw) had so much fun racing with the Indians. And he thought it was, to use his words, a "damn shame they hanged Riel because he was only getting the Indians to stick up for their rights."

When Shaw's father, the late Samuel Shaw, led his family into Western Canada fresh from Kent, England, in 1883, they had to get off the train at what was known as the eleventh siding west of Brandon, Man., because the train didn't go any farther.

So they joined a caravan of carts and set out for Calgary. When they got there his mother found she had no worries about wearing a hat like somebody else, because there was only one other white woman in the place and she wore a shawl.

Mr. Shaw's father had brought over the equipment to set up a woollen mill, his occupation in the Old Country, and he decided Calgary was a nice spot until he had that argument with the council.

He was willing to help Calgary get its industrial legs in return for a two-year tax concession. But the council couldn't see it that way. So when the C.P.R. extended an arm southward to crowd the stage coaches from the Macleod Trail in 1890, Shaw set up his mill at Midnapore. This place which hasn't grown any larger since probably became the first rural area in Alberta to do any manufacturing. The business ended amid great excitement one Easter morning just after the First Great War. The mill burned down.

As son Shaw remembered it, Fish Creek, as it was then known, became Midnapore purely because of one man's fancy. A chap named John Glen, a squatter, was the first postmaster. He somehow carried out his duties despite the fact he could neither read nor write.

This handicap, of course, made his work a trifle difficult. But when the stage brought in the mail from Calgary, Glen would recruit services of the elder Shaw to help him sort the mail.

One day they came across a letter addressed "Postmaster, Midnapore." The thing obviously had got lost on its way to India or somewhere. Well, Mr. Glen handed it back to Mr. Shaw with the remark, "Here, that's you." He then walked out. Shaw became postmaster and Fish Creek became Midnapore.

It was the same John Glen who donated the land upon which the quaint Anglican church stands today. The fact that Glen was a Catholic didn't seem to make much difference. What few Anglicans there were around at the time built the church in 1894. The Catholic church next door was built in 1904.

The Anglican church is an odd looking building and the obvious question is why it was built that way. The answer, said Shaw, is that the Anglicans wanted it that way because it reminded them of their parish churches in England. And so the people would feel still more at home, they brought the bell from England. It still peals over the countryside to call the people to worship and in its call is a tribute to those who sleep in the cemetery beside their church. And if you take the time to browse around you'll find some of the old headstones, the graves encircled by small chain fences, are in themselves something from memory's book.

Most people think of the Riel Rebellion of 1885 as a piece of excitement that sparked the history of Saskatchewan. But big and bluff Hugh Shaw saw service in it from the Alberta side, freighting soldiers and supplies northward from Calgary.

Shaw was trained to handle a rifle, but he said he saw nothing to shoot at. His fondest memory of pioneer strategy was the time a wagon train crossed on a ferry at the Red Deer River and the train's armament—a Gatling gun—was taken over first, leaving the men with nothing to shoot, even if something had appeared.

Shaw struck another match on his trouser leg and his big grey moustache twitched with the humour of the situation even after all those years. He said the only Indian he saw was a friendly Indian and what with either trading or horse racing with them, his service in the rebellion was the best time of his life.

The story of Senator Pat Burns is enough to fill a book itself. His name will live forever in the annals of the ranching industry of the west and for the Alberta traveller, a line of trees near Midnapore stand in his memory. It's a self-made monument, for Burns had them planted. And at Midnapore I met the man who did the work.

For twenty-two years after 1917, William Mayhew was gardener for Burns. Mayhew had become a gardener in

England because of his ability to make great noise with tin pans. His first job was with a man who grew seed and his duties were to pull weeds and frighten the birds. At six a.m. he'd start scaring the birds by rattling tin clappers, banging pans together and hollering like the devil. He said he had to holler, or the old fellow he worked for would soon be hollering at him. Between the two of them, the birds had little peace.

For such professional services Mayhew received four cents a day. When he got a raise to six cents a day and was taking home thirty-six cents a week he figured he was in the big money. So he saved enough to migrate to Calgary in 1912.

It was in 1929 that Mayhew went about the business of planting 1,850 poplars that line the Macleod Trail in the vicinity of Midnapore. The trees that now throw their shadows across the road were only seven feet high when planted and the work took two seasons. One by one, the trees went for five miles south of Calgary's limits, missing the village limits of Midnapore, then continuing for another three miles south. Senator Burns had planned a similar lane on the Banff highway, stretching west from Calgary, but his illness interfered.

Mayhew said the cattle king was a far-sighted man. At De Winton, adjoining Midnapore on the south, he ran some of the trees eastward over a hill so to the traveller they would appear to not suddenly start and just as suddenly end.

Mayhew moved to Midnapore in 1939 and set up his own nursery business and when I met him it was at the time the highway crews were tearing out some of the Burns trees to widen the road. Mayhew said he sat on the steps of his home and watched with tears in his eyes. But he figured it was progress and he was cheered by the fact that as many as possible of the trees were to be saved.

If you'd care for a little side trip—for no particular reason at all, although if it's fall you'll see the most beautiful foothills foliage—turn west a mile or so south of Midnapore and follow gravelled highway No. 19 to Priddis.

It might be worth it. At Priddis you learn how the early

settlers would gather at the forks of water courses and of how from that beginning Alberta eventually became dotted with its towns and villages. Even cities.

Charles Priddis was one of those fellows who had a lot to do with setting the pattern for things to come.

A man from a well-to-do family in Paris, Ontario, Charles Priddis got out west with the survey gangs, but not as one of the men behind the instruments. He looked after the horses.

In 1884 his party set up winter camp at two branches of Fish Creek, a spot which became known as The Forks, about twenty-five miles south-west of Calgary. Charles Priddis liked it so much that he returned in 1886 to file on a homestead, although another man, Jim Ockley, took the honour of being the first to file there the previous year.

But Priddis and Ockley probably chose it for the same reasons. It had wood, water and, heavens above, some coal, which you could say would be the equivalent of steam heat in the days when most people burned buffalo chips.

As a matter of fact there was so much coal around that in time others who followed to Priddis began freighting it clear to Edmonton where it brought $50 a ton, and such adventuresome gentlemen as the traders and police who occupied Edmonton at the time were glad to pay it.

Because of all these factors, other hardy folk began to drift to The Forks and when they had a quorum they got together and named it after Charles Priddis.

Priddis was a typical pioneer. A hardy, good-natured man. He never married, but it was in his cabin that they held the first school and it was he who donated the land for the first school building.

What few changes Priddis has seen in the years have been brought chiefly by nature. At one time the country was quite open and you'll find that hard to understand as you look over the green trees in summer, or note their beauty in fall when they are on the gold standard. Years ago there was little brush and few trees except spruce. After a series of fires, the brush, willows and poplars appeared and when summer is dying their mourning clothes are something to see.

The area has gradually changed from ranching to mixed farming and the sixty-five people who get their mail at the Priddis post office play their part in maintaining southern Alberta's economy.

Just how much, and of what, they ship out is difficult to ascertain because Priddis, like many other interesting Alberta communities, is not on a railway. Inland towns they call them. Even the nearby oil community of Turner Valley is one. So all the produce goes by truck to Calgary. But judging by the amount of grain around Priddis in a good year, there's either a lot of cattle or what there is has a big appetite.

It's just an ordinary village, but somehow it is like a scene from a movie scenario. Perhaps it could tell stories that would make better movie plots than some of the professional Hollywood writers turn out.

Priddis sees many visitors, but none of them these days are rum runners. The community is on what was one of the main trails south in the early days and the rum runners who veered away from the Macleod Trail made the road so busy that at one time the Mounties had a post a couple of miles south of Priddis to direct the traffic, much of it to the local lock-ups.

In Priddis you will find a large, weather-beaten dwelling that for years was a stop-over house between Calgary and the southwest, in the years of stage travel. Priddis is a good hunting area and many prominent Calgary residents can tell stories of the hospitality of the stopping house where they would take their game to be cooked for a virtual banquet, and where they would be entertained by a parrot.

The parrot, it seems, spent its life surprising people with its language. Everybody put up with this for twenty-five years and when they felt they'd heard everything and could no longer be surprised, the parrot laid an egg.

But speaking of stop-over houses, let's go back to the Macleod Trail and the stories of the house on the hill and of the one that used to be in the valley, about fifteen miles south of Calgary.

You can't miss the house on the hill. It's on the west side

of the road. It looks like most farm houses of today, but there's another story under its covers.

The place was built by a man named S. Watson who had a house-warming in 1886. It was taken over a few years later by Albert and Andrew Pratt, great uncles of the present occupant, Murray Anderson.

The house has siding on it today, but under the siding some portions of it are of logs. When it was wired for electricity the crew had great troubles. They had to continually lengthen their bits to drill through the logs. The place has a small cellar which was apparently a part of a bar, the place where the kegs were kept when the stages rolled over the Macleod Trail.

But it is in the valley below the Anderson home where the real stopping house stood. It was there, together with the big stable, until 1951 when it just seemed to disappear over night.

The property was occupied for thirty years by William C. Standish and his good wife. They sold it to some parties who planned to subdivide it into suburban homesites for Calgarians. The Andersons, well in their seventies, then turned to building a new home on the hill.

It's a red, imitation brick place and as he sat enjoying dinner at a table that overlooked the valley where he had farmed amid history for so long, Mr. Standish, a man with a gay beard and equally as gay sense of humour, told me something of what he knew of the old stopping house.

Mr. Standish bought the property in 1920 from the late John Owens, a man who squatted on it years back when people could do that sort of thing without fear of trespass, in the days when the country was a lot more free than it is now and even before arrival of the fences.

Mr. Standish—who knew much of the history hereabouts from his own knowledge, for he'd come out from Bruce County in Ontario with his folks in 1886—said Owens' original stopping place, as a matter of record, was of logs and about sixteen by eighteen feet in size. The travellers slept on blankets on the floor. The place was later enlarged to a house and store, and when Standish bought the property he converted it into a home.

On the east side of the trail, across from the house, there stood a stable, built originally to handle forty head. The driveway was so big that wagons were driven indoors in wet weather. This was built in 1885 and when it was torn down in 1951 it was the first time some people in the district had ever seen a square nail.

Mr. Standish couldn't actually remember his old home when it was a stop-over point, because he was just a young gaffer living not too far away, but he could remember seeing the ox teams pulling the freight wagons from Fort Benton in Montana to Calgary over the old trail.

Standish went back over the years and painted a visual picture of twenty steers pulling the great wagons with their high wheels. It must have been a tremendous sight and, as Mr. Standish said, was accompanied by a great deal of noise. One could hear the wagon trains coming for miles. The big tires cut a furrow six inches deep in the prairie sod and one wagon never used the track of the other.

As the streamliner whips past the lumbering freight trains of today, the overland stage of those days was the elite in fast travel. What they called Concord Coaches rattled their jogging way along the Macleod trail.

The coach hung on leather straps instead of springs and six people rode inside and about four on the roof. The fare was the same, inside or out. The driver had time to keep and the four spanking horses whipped the carriage over the prairie at ten miles an hour.

Things weren't so fast but they were a lot cheaper along the Macleod Trail in those days. When his old home was torn down Mr. Standish came across some account books, used when Owens had operated the store.

The yellowing, brittle pages which Standish treasures showed that on January 5, 1891, one G. Kennie bought six bars of soap, a sack of flour, one cream of tartar, three plugs of chewing tobacco and seven pounds of bacon for the princely sum of $5.55.

Farmers then were getting ten cents for eggs and nine cents for butter. Ginger snaps seemed to be the chief dessert.

One account in the books showed Kennie, who was a good customer, bought a suit of clothes for $6 and an overcoat for $8.50, and the entry prompted Mr. Standish to comment in his shy, humorous way that the overcoat, being of such good material and so high priced, must surely have come from England.

In many respects Standish to me typified the old-time Albertan. He told me the reason he felt so good was because he'd always had lots to eat, chiefly good Alberta beef although lately they were selling stuff that was too young, to his way of thinking.

No publicity man today could make Albertans too proud of their beef. They have grown up with it and they know its worth. Its citizens, large and small, have a big stake in their Province and they are happy for their visitors to have a good steak on it.

The worth of Alberta beef has been known for years back and it was Mrs. Standish who remembered the story of the Calgary butcher of years ago who approached the parents of a very fat boy to have the boy sit in his shop window along with a sign: "Fed on Alberta beef." The parents refused. The son grew up to be a C.P.R. engineer.

But it was a little difficult to pull away from the Standish home for this jovial chap was full of stories about changes. The biggest, he had noticed, he said, seemingly getting ready to duck, was in Mrs. Standish.

There was a merry twinkle in his eye as he looked across the table at his good wife and mate for so many years and said, "Well, when I got married my wife could wear my hatband as a belt. And look at her now." Mrs. Standish, really a very trim woman, just smiled as if it was an old joke.

But the old trail has sure changed. Today Mr. and Mrs. Standish can't look out of the window at any hour of the day or night but what a car is going by. And one of them is ours. So let's get going.

As we move on southward one can't help but feel that

the real boardwalk of Canada is the station platform in the country towns. Just picture the towns ahead of us toward Macleod, such places as High River, Nanton, Stavely; and along a branch line a few miles to the east, Vulcan, Champion, Carmangay.

They are alike as two peas in a pod, generally speaking. But in the days of development their station platforms were the theatres of great and changing dramas.

The station platforms were no sooner laid than courageous people stepped from them to scatter like the wind, open up the country and get the big show underway. And for Alberta it has been a terrific performance. From coal to cattle; from wheat on dry land to peas and sugar beets on irrigated soil. The Province has made its living from what could be grazed from the top of the soil or what could be grown in its top six inches, and now it's going down thousands of feet to bring up its oil and its gas for further riches and more industry.

But the stage for it all has been the station platform and all manner of actors have trod its footboards. Where the talking pictures replaced the vaudeville, the highways today are carrying some of the load that was once the exclusive burden of the railways, but the station platform is still the biggest stage of life.

In some places the mad antics of nature—coupled with some bad farming practices by actors who did not know their lines—left the station boardwalk a forlorn place—a cold place, like an unused theatre.

But there are just as many other places where it resounds to the tramp of eager feet as another generation of actors in the costumes of different countries come as a chorus of immigrants to win with the west. And for those people, Alberta, with all its resources, today looks like the place to place the bets.

Throughout the years the station platforms of Alberta—and the other Provinces—have not exactly mirrored life, as the saying goes. They are a little too wrinkled themselves to do that. But they have certainly felt life. So the platform is like any stage. It only feels things. The people on it express them.

As the Alberta show has gone on through the years, the stage has seldom enjoyed full brilliance because the headlight of the train is fleeting. The real spotlight has been from the little squares of light reflected from the coach windows, dancing along the platform just as the spotlight dances on the stage.

And the actors have been living people and just as nervous as any make-believe hero on any stage as they stepped from the wings of the cars and into that little square of light and faced the unknown and, as often as not, some pretty severe critics.

When they stepped from the stage as the première was over, it was to either make their way or lose it, but the station boardwalk continued to hold a fascination as a promenade. And its importance in the show that followed depended upon the production of the people. If they farmed a lot and shipped a lot or did a great business in the town, it was a long boardwalk. But if it was a small show it was only a small stage.

Sometimes and in some places the people at the box office —the railways—weren't too sure just how big the show would be. So to be on the safe side they extended the stage with a cinder path. Something like having some spare chairs in the back of the hall.

But all of the community's life walked the stage. The young toddlers came down to watch the unending drama of the daily show when the train came in. They looked in fascination at the chief actor, the engineer, or were clucked under the chin by the prompter, the jovial conductor. And when the show was over for the day, the kids stopped to pick up the flattened coins and nails they had put on the tracks and happily raced uptown with splinters in their bare feet.

As the kids grew older the stage took on different aspects. It was sorrowful as they left amid the applause of the family and friends for the broader stage of life. Or maybe the stage was shrouded in gloom as they left in uniforms of their country, bound from the mezzanine of the land to pacify the gods of war in a bitter performance that somebody always wants to repeat. And no stage was ever brighter than the station platform the day they came back.

Life still moves across the boardwalks of Alberta's country stations and the scene shifters are the fellows who haul the little wagons from the freight and express sheds to the train car doors.

It's always the same play and, day after day, the scenery is the same . . . bread boxes, milk cans, newspapers, machinery parts. But the actors change. And that brings Okotoks to mind.

Okotoks always reminds me of an old opera house.

Its buildings have the same nostalgia about them as has an old and disused theatre. Okotoks has seen a great many plays, a great many different players and itself has taken part in a few acts. Now, much as the legitimate theatre gave way to the talkies, it lives with its memories.

Okotoks, about twenty-five miles south of Calgary, is still busy with its own affairs and by no means actually a ghost of its former self. It has shared the fate of all towns, however, that grew up within the shadows of cities. Or tried to grow up.

In its heydey its long platform at the depot, where nine men once worked, was a jumping off point not only for settlement of the farm and ranch country around it, but for Alberta's first oil development. It was to Okotoks that the drilling equipment and the men to man it came and assembled themselves for the 17-mile haul to Turner Valley behind 12- and 16-horse teams.

Turner Valley is the granddaddy of not only Alberta's but also Canada's oil industry. But like granddad it doesn't get around so much these days. It isn't so active. Its thunder has been stolen by some husky youngsters up around Leduc and Redwater and Woodbend.

So Okotoks is like a grandfather beginning to show its years. But it still manages to have fun along Sheep Creek where its wooded picnic and sports ground is a Sunday mecca for many Calgarians.

The old-timers around Okotoks can tell of the days when the town had three hotels. But that's a story you can pick up in most of the prairie towns. A story of great activity during the West's shakedown cruise. In those days the settlers came to town early to be sure of getting a room for the night and a spot to stable their horses. They made their fun where they found it and with Scotch whiskey at $1.50 for 26 ounces, some of it wasn't too expensive.

Sheep Creek then was a log run. There was a millpond on the west side of town and John Lineham's sawmill sold lumber to the homesteaders at $10 a thousand feet.

To the west, out in what became the oil fields, another place bustled and it was called Black Diamond. Its settlers skated on Sheep Creek and lighted the gas that seeped from the crevices along the river bank but they gave little thought to the potentialities. But when Turner Valley began to develop in 1913, there was a great rush to get on the band-wagon.

The settlers came first. Many of them were what became known as remittance men from the Old Country. But for all of their reputation in later years they were the backbone of the country, and in many cases their remittances were what kept money flowing in their communities.

Land around Black Diamond was available at $3 an acre if the homesteader put water on it, for there was great talk of irrigation. But it was also a great problem, for the new-comers knew nothing of farming, at least many of them didn't, let alone how to make water work for them.

They knew little of the lay of the land and it was quite some time before many discovered the reason their irrigation projects weren't doing so well was because they were trying to make water flow up hill.

Black Diamond got its name because of the coal and coke that was developed there in the eighties by Harry Dinning. The commodity was shipped by team to Calgary.

The fellows who gave this part of the country and its homesteaders their first real start were a couple of English chaps—Eric Buckler and a Captain Gilson, both killed in the first war. They did it by the simple expedient of going into the dairy business, importing cows from Quebec and selling them to homesteaders on a cream share basis.

They kept about sixty head themselves and in true traditions of the English sportsman—everybody had a pony and polo was a great game—it was quite common on occasion to hear the hunting horn blown for a jolly chappie in a red coat to ride out to get the cows.

Old-timers like Dick Spackman, who ranched in the hills around 1911, recall stories of great times among neighbours who today would be called characters, not because of their type but because of their individualities. A report that there was a mouse in somebody's pantry, Spackman told me, was as likely as not to mean a rallying to the gun rack, everybody getting their rifles and engaging in a big game hunt for the mouse that didn't have a chance.

Black Diamond and Turner Valley today, within two miles of each other, offer the traveller who takes the new black top road a sight that to the oil industry is as much a part of history as the threshing machine is to farming. It's the sight of derricks rearing their weather-beaten heads from the plains and clinging to the hillsides. The place was once virtually a forest of derricks.

Alberta is one of the few Provinces that is doing something to tell the traveller, by roadway signs, just what he is looking at. The Industrial Development Board is marking important present-day sites within the Province, and their attractive marker near Okotoks gives you a quick look at Turner Valley's past.

It was Alberta's first major oil field and since oil was discovered in 1914, or a trace of it then, the field has yielded well over 100,000,000 barrels of crude.

Until 1947, when the Edmonton area fields hit the world's headlines, Turner Valley had produced over 90 per cent of Canada's oil. One well in six years gave nearly 1,000,000 barrels of naphtha. During the Second Great War the valley made a tremendous contribution to the Allied cause. It fed the fuel-short armies with 53,500,000 barrels of crude oil.

The oil industry will pay tribute to Turner Valley for a great many years to come. Its crown passed to Leduc-Woodbend-Redwater after 1948 but it began to die in early old age because of the poor conservation methods of its infancy. There are those today who believe its life could be extended another twenty years with possible recovery by today's secondary recovery methods of thirty million barrels of crude. But because of the lack of conservation know-how in the field's youth no matter what its total yield, it would be only a limited percentage of the total content of the reservoir. Alberta has learned a valuable lesson from letting Turner Valley shoot its bolt too quickly.

The field's history has been varied since wet gas was first discovered in 1913. Signs of light oil brought a mad scramble of investors the following year. About 490 companies were organized and about 44 began drilling, so a great many people, too, learned valuable but costly lessons.

When the first Great War broke out the flame of hate in Europe also seared and broke the valley's big bubble and by 1916 only twenty drilling outfits and two small refineries were at work in the valley.

About 1926 another boom came. Some early companies were revived and new ones formed. Ten years later the first real production of crude was obtained. The valley became so busy two communities were known as Little Chicago and Little New York. The valley hit its peak to help win the war but since has been steadily declining. It has been, however, and still is an important producer of natural gas. Although it was first located in 1913, it was not until 1924 that gas was developed in volume, enough to begin supplying many communities in southwestern Alberta, including Calgary. The field for twelve years enjoyed a rôle as a naphtha producer and the amount of natural gas wasted in flares was tremendous. These flares lighting the night sky became a sight that drew passengers to windows of trains passing through Calgary.

In 1950 it was estimated that the valley's natural gas reserves amounted to 251 billion cubic feet. The wastage had been reduced because of greater development of markets and the repressuring of the valley by pumping the gas back into the field.

For the layman there is in the valley an interesting sight that in some respects is a reminder of nature's actions in the days when all of Alberta's great underground resources were being created.

It stands in a field about midway between Okotoks and the oilfields, like a lonely, bewildered giant known locally as the "big rock."

At a casual glance it looks like a huge house without windows. Closer examination shows it to be quartzite of tremendous size. Just why nature left it there alone, apart from a few smaller pieces some distance away, is something that never will be answered.

But before we get lost at the crossroads—intersecting roads in the valley carry posts with a dozen or more markers pointing to well sites—let's leave the valley and get back to the Macleod Trail and southward to High River.

Here's the ranching West. Here's yesterday and today rubbing shoulders on Main Street.

Here's where Johnson, the jeweller, advertises fine English china on a sign adjacent to one decorated with cattle brands which Bradley uses to advertise a western welcome and, of course, leather goods.

Here's where seven grain elevators attest to the community's productivity but where the big, for a small town, fairgrounds, with long wooden grandstand and bleachers and the stock chutes, shows where its heart remains. Out on the open range.

This is the place where the country's leading commentator of Canadiana, John Fisher, once stood on the highway, looked to the foothills and mountains on the west, to the sweep of plains on the east, came to the conclusion you'd never see anything like it anywhere.

In the late eighties this country was littered with buffalo bones and Levi Bradley—the leather goods man—remembered it well. In 1891, along about the time the Calgary-Macleod railway was coming through, he helped collect the bones. With wagons, men roamed from Okotoks to Stavely and from the foothills to the prairies. They hauled bones by the wagon-load to the railway grade, and when tracks were put on the grade the bones were hauled east to be made into fertilizer.

It was just one of the many jobs for the young men of High River of the day. Breaking sod with two horses and a plow with a fourteen-inch blade and getting $2.50 an acre for it was another. When the farmers began arriving, the Bradley family, for one, turned to leather and at one time bought leather ten rolls at a time, each roll weighing 200 pounds, and had five people working all winter making harness.

But before that there was another breed. The cattleman. High River saw its birth with the famous Bar-U ranch which once ran 40,000 head. The first animals were trailed in from Idaho in 1882. It was a big ranch on a big range that saw its first fence when the Canadian Pacific Railway enclosed its main line right-of-way nearly forty miles to the north.

Those days have gone but the colour remains and the visitor can find it in the dress of the people of High River. There was a time when a cowboy bought a pair of boots to cover his feet, but now many of them get boots that cover the country like a sunset. The flowers that bloom in the spring also blossom on the saddles but the fellow who went around hell-bent-for-leather, as the range saying goes, now bounces on foam rubber. Years ago a fellow rode with his horse, now he is cushioned to the bounce. Foam rubber pads make his days on the range that much more comfortable. Today the High River cowboy likes a hand-tooled and flower-stamped saddle.

Here the visitor will find window shopping that measures up to the illustrations in the old western stories. He'll find saddles and gun scabbards, arm bands and bandannas—and in the next window, fine china.

He'll find people who wear western garb, associated usually with movies, because it is part of their every-day life and, too, it is comfortable. It takes the visitor an hour or two to acclimatize himself to the sight of men in high heeled shoes and leg-fitting blue jeans. But unlike the visitor, who may come from Ontario and be sporting a colourful summer shirt stamped in a Hawaiian motif, they are not playing.

To these people it is everyday dress, in one form or another. And they pay good money for what they wear. A fellow with riding boots of bright yellow and trimmed with bright green goes unnoticed on High River's streets of a Saturday night. The man with the pair that are all green with the rough side of the leather on the outside may look colourful, but that's his business and he probably paid fifty bucks for the privilege.

There was a time when such trappings marked the drug store cowboy, but no longer. Today the men who actually ride the range are inclined to "doll up." But they still buy for serviceability, and when their bright things get scuffed they wear them to work, just as you do with your shiny old blue suit.

So it's hardly a place where you'd expect to find nylon in demand. But in his little home down at the auto camp, an old-time cowboy, Hope Hunter—who in summer has for his neighbour Guy Weadick, the man who originated the term Stampede for the famous Calgary show—has made a good thing out of making nylon lariats, bull and horse leads, halters, breast collars, men's dress belts, even harness for children.

Hunter, who was born on a Priddis ranch and rode in the Calgary Stampede when he was fourteen, is probably the only man in the country who has "hung one," to use a phrase, on a Mountie and got away with it. From his little factory he has turned out lanyards of nylon that are worn by Mounted Policemen across Canada.

Hunter got his idea first when he saw nylon parachute cord on sale in hardware stores for use as clotheslines. It occurred to him it would make good rope. But it was lifeless. So he developed a formula to stiffen the nylon and that's his trade secret.

His nylon ropes have been used by contestants in the

Calgary Stampede, where any rope gets the toughest of tests. They are used by cowboys on the range. And the men have faith in them, for Hunter once tied a rope between two tractors, told the drivers to haul away. The rope didn't break.

Of course the visitor may not get to meeting these people. Or their neighbours like Billy Henry who in 1898 took 180 head of beef cattle by train from High River to Vancouver, then by boat and overland trail to the Yukon to feed the prospectors and establish the name of Pat Burns in the meat industry in those parts.

But there's no reason why the visitor can't see the Canadian Pacific Railway station. And upon seeing it, he may wonder why High River should rate such a depot of sandstone. There's a great story behind the High River that used to be behind the depot, but is now all around it, and there's a story behind the depot, too.

In 1911 Calgary outgrew its sandstone depot. It was torn down, block by block, shipped to High River and rebuilt. What didn't go into the High River depot went farther south and you'll find it today at Claresholm.

High River—which is a natural name for a town on the banks of the Highwood River—will never forget its past, but yet it keeps in step with the present. It's hard for any community of similar size to match the High River community centre. The interest the town takes in welfare of its young people has made it a leader in that field, so much so that a western Canadian conference of 'teen age groups was held there. The adults were brought up under the same atmosphere and many contend that is why High River is such a neighbourly place in which to live.

This town of the big hat remembers and honours the people who made it. In its George Lane Memorial Park, High River has a sanctuary of trees and lawn where a fellow can find a little rest with a book on a pleasant summer evening, or perhaps a quiet picnic with the family.

At the entrance, cattle brands cover the posts which hold a plaque. It's a plain board and on it is stamped, "In memory of George Lane, 1856-1925, pioneer Alberta stockman. He gave this park to the people of High River district."

Lane came to Alberta in 1884 in charge of a herd of trail cattle from the United States and became manager, later owner of the Bar-U. He saw it grow from the days its beef fed the crews that pushed the steel across the prairies and into the mountains.

And up on the peak of old Mount Rae, due northwest, there is another plaque. This one the visitor will never see, but if he knows of it he'll have a better understanding of the western fellowship that exists among the young men who walk the streets of High River.

In the summers many of the young men like to ride over the foothills and then scale and conquer the high peaks that rise behind them. Robert Cousins was one of these.

But young Cousins' spirit of adventure was stilled by an accident in 1948. The next summer some of his young friends scaled Mount Rae, rearing 10,576 feet, and on its bonnet they placed a brass plaque. They then lit a fire to signal the folks at home so far below that they had reached their objective. And the flickering flame illuminated the words on the plaque: "To the memory of Robert Walter Cousins, our pal Cuzzy, who died in an aircraft accident Dec. 26, 1948. He stands beside us on the highest peak."

Those are the kind of people who made High River, and those are the kind who keep it alive.

About twenty-five miles south-west of the town, along a gravelled road, the visitor can journey to see the EP Ranch, western home of the Duke of Windsor.

On the way the visitor comes to the South Fork Trading Post. There are sheep, deer, buffalo, elk and goat horns and skulls above the door on the outside, and in the inside there is young Alfred Baines, son of the founder of this picturesque post, and he'll drop anything to argue that the Canadian government should preserve more of the country's historical sites.

If you have the time and inclination, young Baines will suggest taking you out to show you just what he means. Where he will want to take you, on horseback, will be into the hills about fourteen miles to the west. He'll show you what he figures only about a dozen white men have seen: paintings on rocks. They are in dark red pigment that has weathered the years and Baines figures if a fellow could find the secret of it, he'd make a fortune selling it to farmers to paint barns.

It's pretty hard to determine just what some of the pictures represent. Some are definitely animals. They are drawn as a child would do them, in straight lines. The Indians around the post, he said, were superstitious about the paintings. They believed they were done by little hermits who live in the mountains.

Baines, of course, sees nothing unusual in the very place where he lives. The log trading post to where the ranchers and the Indians come to sit on the counter, or stand with backs to the warm, pot-belly stove, and barter for their needs, and where on occasion, the Duke and Duchess of Windsor visit.

The South Fork Trading Post, on the south fork of the Highwood River, sits by itself in a grand sweep of valley. It looks today as it did when Phil Weinard hauled the logs from the hills and built it in 1919 for Baines' father, the late Harry Baines.

It looks the same, that is, except for the gas pump.

The nearest competitors are twelve miles to the north and eight to the south. The mountains are on the west and High River twenty miles to the east. And quite a number of the people in between go there to pick up their mail for the post is also the Pekisko Post Office.

Young Baines has spent all his life there, apart from the time he spent with the air force. His father died in 1924, his mother in 1949. So today, a good-looking man in the comfortable garb of the range country, Alfred Baines runs the post. And he says that apart from the fact prices go up and down, things have been much the same in all the time he's been there. The stock is the same type and the Indians still like the colourful prints for dresses.

Baines' mother collected Indian curios. She sold one

collection to a museum in Montreal. Baines has boxes of stuff in the place and now that the tourists are beginning to wander farther from the main roads and get off the beaten track, he plans to put the curios on display. So we may call back.

In the meantime, let's be along. Let's go back to the Macleod Trail. Let's move on southward, paced by the glorious sunset in the west. Through Nanton: The friendliest town in the friendly West, so it says, proudly. Also the home of a restaurant that served a top sirloin steak, accompanied by good, nourishing Scotch broth, for $1.25.

On down to Claresholm, the first rural centre in Alberta to build a swimming pool, the work of the Men's Club, whose officers say that a good men's club, representative of all branches of the community, can do more than a service club in a small town because service clubs are restricted by their categories.

If you care to stop there's Rainbow and Cutthroat trout on Willow and Lyndon creeks to the west. In the fall there are deer and elk "over the gap," thirty miles west into the mountains. Go twenty-three miles by car then any rancher will take you the rest of the way by jeep or wagon. Set up your tent, camp out for four days or so, have your fun, maybe get your bag, then the rancher will come back and pick you up. But make all arrangements before hand.

Before we leave Claresholm, let's look at the war memorial the town's Col. Lyndon Chapter of the I.O.D.E. erected in 1951. It's a stone cairn, of the type used by the Historic Sites and Monuments Board to mark Canada's historical spots. The stones were gathered locally, and the work was done by Frank Peters, a bricklayer and not a stonemason, according to a blueprint obtained from Ottawa.

The memorial pays tribute to the community's thirty-six dead of two wars, and an interesting point about it is that Peters obtained the stones from a farm occupied by his son-in-law, Clarence Travis, out nearby Granum way. Travis married Winnifred Peters shortly after the Peters family arrived in Claresholm in 1949 from Dorking, Surrey, England. The reason the Peters moved to Alberta was because another daughter, Phyllis, had married Lawrence Cotter, a Canadian soldier, in Surrey. Cotter farms seventeen miles west of Claresholm.

When Peters migrated with his family, little did he think or realize that he would go to his daughter's farm to get stones to fashion a memorial to men who'd made the trip the other way but didn't return to a country that for Peters is now home.

So we go on to Macleod, and, theoretically at least, the end of the Macleod Trail. Theoretically, that is, because the trail continues southward, through the big Blood Indian reserve, through the town of Cardston, from where it jogs to the west to Waterton National Park—a border straddling peace park—and another branch to Carway, where you enter the United States.

Perhaps we should skip down there for a look-see. You may like to experience the strange, eerie loneliness as the car rolls over the Blood reserve. It's the largest in Canada, 353,448 acres, or 540 square miles, populated by 1,925 Indians.

It's like being in another man's country. The foothills have dropped to a mere rise and the mountains, topped by Old Chief, curtain the west. To the east the everlasting prairie remains. When you top rises and look southward, you feel you can see clear to Arizona.

Log and frame homes and here and there a tent—with radio aerial outside—dot the wide landscape. Outside these Indian homes are the inevitable democrat, the hay rack, but outside many, too, are late model cars and big trucks.

The spire of a lonely Anglican church rises above a hill and the white peaks in the background make the scene appear to have been transplanted from Switzerland.

In the centre of the reserve the tall grass grows around a cemetery protected from everything but the wind, of which there is plenty, by a wire fence. The tombstones recall the lives of Bruised Head, 1876-1950, and Kate Red Crow, 1889-1950, and others of their people.

Outside the cemetery a huge concrete memorial, surrounded by a small white picket fence, tells another story in cryptic engraving:

> Peace forever.
>
> In loving memory of Head Chief Red Crow. Born 1830. Died 1900. Signed treaty No. 7, 1877. His successor Head Chief Crop Eared Wolf. Born 1846. Died 1913. And all who rest here.

It was Indian treaty No. 7, signed Sept. 22, 1877, that saw the surrender of 50,000 square miles of Indian territory in the south-west corner of Alberta.

And down at Cardston we meet those who were among the first to make their homes in Alberta. Cardston was settled by men and women from Utah in 1886. They came under leadership of Charles Ora Card and the Church of Jesus Christ of Latter-Day Saints. Or, as better known, the Mormons. They were irrigationists, and the story of how they helped to develop southern Alberta by irrigation rightfully belongs with the history of Lethbridge, which we come to when we travel the big ditch.

Cardston, snuggled in a valley, offers the visitors the only Mormon temple in Canada. A huge building constructed in 1913 at a cost of $800,000 it is made of white granite imported from Vernon, B.C. It is, as a matter of fact, the only Mormon temple on British soil. There are six others on this continent —all in the United States—and one in Hawaii, but no two are alike.

You may see the temple, wander its spacious grounds, be told of its history by guides who are there all summer, but you may not enter unless you are a member in good standing of the church. Without going into the history of the church, that means you must be a member who refrains from use of liquor, tobacco, tea and coffee. You must be of good morals, be a regular attendant at services and pay tithing, or ten per cent of your net annual income to the church. There's no objection should you go dancing.

It took ten years to finish the building, chiefly because it was quite a job to cut the stone by hand on the site. Somebody later got the idea of cutting it by machinery at Vernon. After it was completed, it took two years to finish the murals.

Before it was dedicated, in 1923, anybody could inspect the inside. But since its dedication that privilege has been granted only to two who are not members of the church. They were the Earl of Bessborough and Lord Tweedsmuir during their respective terms as Governor-General.

So let's return to Macleod, a place you can wrap up as part and parcel of the entire Canadian west. It is regrettable that the strings are a little loose. Macleod, so far as any Canadian officialdom is concerned, seems to be neither yesterday nor tomorrow. It in itself lives for today and what it has of yesterday grows a little more weatherbeaten, a little more ramshackle as each day passes.

Oh, there's the usual cairn, the usual writing on stone to mark Macleod's historical niche, but nothing is done about the few buildings still remaining that have weathered the years since 1874. The town in 1952 was beginning to show some interest in its past and the name was changed back to Fort Macleod.

It was in October of that year that the North-West Mounted Police established Fort Macleod after what the history and guide books, in a priceless understatement, describe as an "arduous march of 1,000 miles" across the prairies.

The Mounties, as nearly everybody must know by now, brought law and order to a lawless country in the days when lawlessness meant trading whisky to the Indians for furs and odds and ends of considerable value. The coming of the Mounties actually made possible the later settlement of the country, the birth of its cities, towns, villages.

The Mounties, after that arduous march, built their first fort on an island immediately to the northeast of the present town of Macleod. It seemed like a good idea at the time, but the changing current of Oldman River made it difficult to get in or out—or on or off, whichever applies to an island.

So the police went back to high and dry land, moved their

fort buildings to what is now the townsite. And there some of them stand. And nothing is done about it. On the river bank—behind the main street—there is a log shack that was part of the fort. Today it is some citizen's tool shed. There's another place uptown that is somebody's home, all neatly fixed up. Near the tool shed down by the river there's another long, log building with logs that have square ends. It, too, came from the island. In the years it has been a procession of things, including a drug store and a post office. When I saw it in 1951 it was full of sawdust and a sign outside said: "Ice for sale."

Adjacent to the highway on the west skirt of the town remains all that is left of the force's second and last home in Macleod. This place was the officers' mess. Until 1951 there were a couple of stables on the property, too, but they burned.

This one building now sits alone, listening to the song of the telephone wires strung along the highway, the roar of tires on blacktop and soughing of the wind in the naked looking trees that have been there as long as it.

Most of its windows stare vacantly at life today and those that are boarded give it the appearance from some angles of the patched eye of a pirate. Vines climb the porch when the weather is good for climbing and in the fall they rustle in death.

A tobacco company has advertising on the walls. Instead of a piece of Canadiana the building looks like a farm house deserted by a man who couldn't make a go of it and who tried to pick up a few bucks by selling space on the building walls.

You can enter through the white porch facing the east, where the officers sat of an evening enjoying and shooting the breeze, but the interior corridors are a litter of paper, broken boards and doors leaning every way. It's rather a sad sight and few stop to inspect it. Not because it is so depressing, but because there's nothing there to tell them what it is, anyway. And just how long it would remain was problematical. The town in the winter of 1951-52 sold the building to a railway sectionman for $400. The buyer intended to tear it down and use the lumber to build a home.

But all of the loose strings have been tightened in the centre of Macleod today. It's not as effective, of course, when the real thing is available, but in its community centre Macleod has honoured its history and, incidentally, set up a few of its public services.

The community centre, of a full block with a chipped rock fence on one side, was converted from a bare prairie lot. It has the attractive homes of the post office, courthouse, provincial telephone exchange. There stands the town's cenotaph, a tablet commemorating the march of the Mounties. There the citizens may go to swim, curl and skate as the seasons call. There they may bowl on green lawns. They also have a nice golf course, out west of town on the site of the old police pasture.

And this beautiful centre which Macleod has been quietly developing for years, with the help of the Province and Dominion, is known as Col. Macleod Memorial Park, after Col. J. F. Macleod, CMG., the man who led the mounties and gave the fort its name.

Macleod, with palisades at each highway entrance, lives up to its frontier history in the architecture of its buildings. And a frame building on the walls of which is a big sign advertising the occupant as a "wheelwright" helps, too. Although the occupant, Claude Stevens, says it's many a year since he's been called upon to fix a wagon wheel. Today he fixes cabinets.

3

Over the Crow

So LET's go over the Crowsnest Pass.

A pretty name, isn't it? A rugged name, too. A name that implies country of crag and canyon, the beauties of nature in the rough and a country of high adventure. The Crowsnest Pass lives up to its name. This is a country of coal, a country of great beauty in the summer, a country being developed for its fine skiing in winter. It is a country of Indian wars of years ago and now of Indian lore to fill the notebooks of the vacationing historians whose base camps today are amid the comforts of the many guest or "dude" ranches in the foothills.

It is a country of great mountain tragedy, for here the visitor finds the awesome sight of a once beautiful valley that was covered by 100 feet of tumbling mountain rock within 100 seconds, the story, in brief, of the great slide that buried the town of Frank in 1903.

It is not a long road. Something around 60 miles westward from the time you leave the junction of the main highways at Macleod until you are over the Crowsnest Pass, at an altitude of 4,449 feet, one of the lowest passes in the Canadian Rockies, and entering British Columbia. But it is an important road. On the maps it is known as No. 3 highway. By name it is the Trans-Provincial Highway. But the people who live along it, and plug hard for it, know it as the Southern

Trans-Canada Highway. That is a name of their choosing. But they are not wrong. The road, which connects with Medicine Hat at the east end, will take you westward into Vancouver, or southward to Spokane and over to the western United States.

The road is the lower bar of a square of roads that run along the foothills northward to Edmonton then west into Jasper and southward again through the mountains. It is the southern running mate to the Trans-Canada Highway proper that runs from Medicine Hat, after entering Alberta, westward to Calgary and then into the mountains.

A mile or so west of Macleod is the junction of the highways running north, south, east and west. Here the Alberta government in tourist season maintains an information office. An attractive log-type building on a knoll, it is on a happily-chosen site that presents Alberta in one complete vista. The sight from this bureau–lush, rolling land to the north; endless plains to the east and south and the barrier of mountains to the west–is a welcome to the Province that was written by nature and could never be duplicated, probably not even adequately described by the typewriters of the men who write tourist promotion.

This area to the west of Macleod is old, and yet it is new. Just west of Macleod you can drive off the beaten track and into the hills where the Indians drove the buffalo to slaughter. To entice them to the kill, as a man today uses a decoy duck, they would wear the hides of coyotes, attract the attention of the buffalo by crawling on hands and knees before the great herds. This is an area that proudly proclaims itself as the home of Alberta's first homesteader, a swash-buckling world adventurer by the name of John George Brown who has gone down in Alberta's history as Kootenai Brown. He passed through this country as a youth in his twenties in 1865 and so liked what he saw that he returned two years later to remain until his death in the twenties.

From Macleod you roll westward through the Piegan Indian reservation, a wide expanse of country made wider and more expansive by its flat roof of blue sky. Life moves quietly on the reserve. The buckboards jog across the prairie to the isolated homes and nothing seems to be in a hurry—not even the fleecy white clouds, that add the fourth dimension of depth to this presentation of nature.

It is that way at Pincher Station. A man can stand with a crowd of people on the platform of Pincher Station and be so awed by the scene before him that he is left absolutely alone. Not lonely, mind you. Just alone. As an old cowhand once put it to me: "I stood there one day and I had the feeling there was nothing in this world but me and that bit of country." Cowhands as a rule are not poetic. Nor are policemen. But a member of the North-West Mounted Police, as it was known when it came to this land in 1874, wrote in his journal, with reference to this corner of southern Alberta, "One of the most attractive, interesting and romantic in the territory."

To see that romance alive even today, all a man has to do is to drive three miles south of Pincher Station to the town of Pincher Creek. If Pincher Creek had been born in Nevada during the gold rush, instead of in Alberta in the days before the open range was laced with corsets of barbed wire, it would have been known as Pincher City.

Pincher Creek is that kind of a place. It is the kind of a place that has the battered, wind and sun-tanned features of the west. It has a face that is strong in character even though you see it only in profile. No matter how you look at Pincher Creek, you see only its profile.

You can get there by train, but the train, of course, stops at Pincher Station. You can get there on good hard-surfaced roads, but they bypass it. You could fly over it, but then you would probably miss it in the beauties of the Rockies that protect and shelter it and the valley where it nestles and where, some citizens will tell you with a straight face, they once had a winter without frost.

Others, with some thought, are inclined to doubt this. They say their friends must be referring to the winter when it was so mild Pincher Creek's citizens found it tough to make ice. But in Pincher Creek and its people, there lives the old west. It is there not only in spirit, but in body, too. It is a peculiar place whose citizens relish the past, look to the future, but do not worry too much about today. To say that in another era it would have been known as Pincher City is not too much of a stretch of the imagination, either. Many who are there went there because they thought it was going to be bigger than Calgary, some 130 miles to the north. It did not grow that big and never will, but in its old age it is just as healthy.

As a matter of fact, Pincher Creek is older than Calgary. It lays claim to being one of the oldest communities west of Winnipeg. It does not say this to annoy Macleod, thirty miles to the east. Its citizens admit that the Mounties in their westward march stopped at Macleod in 1874. But they argue it was Pincher Creek that had the hay. And in the vernacular of these times, it still has hay and plenty of it.

Take the Pincher Creek Community Auction Sales Limited. It began business about 1945 with an old typewriter. In six years it grew to 1,100 members, ranchers whose holdings run for miles around. But if they ever got a fair-sized quorum at head office the place would collapse. The association handles sale of cattle by community auctions at strategic centres around Pincher Creek and it does an annual business of $3,000,000 but its bookwork is done in an old building that was once a hotel, then a rooming house and at the moment is on the condemned list. This big business is done under the watchful eye of Arthur E. Ryan, the secretary-treasurer, who was a bank manager and who happened to be stationed in Pincher Creek when retirement age came and who stayed there because "nobody ever left."

In Pincher Creek today you can talk with men who helped open the west. The numbers of those who came from the east and trekked overland from end of steel at, say, Medicine Hat, are growing fewer although Pincher Creek claims it lists more men and women of such distinction than any other community in the Province.

You can get first-hand stories of opening of the west from the West's sons and daughters who were born at Pincher Creek, or moved there as children, and the history is living forever in the poetry of one of the town's businessmen, A. L. (Scotty) Freebairn, who runs a ladies ready-to-wear shop in the daytime and of an evening writes rough and tough poetic words about his old friends and the old days. What Robert W. Service did for the sourdough, Freebairn has done in his quiet way for the ranchers, the police, Indians and the range and homestead land they settled and the mountains they conquered.

Freebairn was eighteen when he joined his father at Pincher Creek in 1899. The father had come from Scotland seventeen years before to help build telegraph shacks as the C.P.R. hammered its way across the country. The reason Freebairns went to Pincher Creek was because they were told that some day it would be bigger than Calgary. It was all a dream, of course, and the people have given up dreaming, but they have not given up hope of growth. With hundreds of thousands of dollars being poured into its natural gas possibilities, Pincher Creek is still in step with the rest of Alberta.

Pincher Creek is the focal point of an area that has considerable economic importance as a gas-condensate field. Exploration was still comparatively limited when it was estimated that its gas reserves amounted to 1,583,600,000,000 cubic feet. Locked with this was an anticipated 35,000,000 barrels of light crude oil and about 5,250,000 long tons of sulphur. Development, with Canadian Gulf Oil Company leading the field, depended upon future expansion of the natural gas market.

But the people of Pincher Creek say there is nothing new in all this. That is when they get around to telling the story of Kootenai Brown, the first man to settle in southern Alberta and, of course, at Pincher Creek, where else?

Brown's early history is rather sketchy. It is tied up with the days when nobody asked questions of his neighbours, consequently little was handed down. In appearance he was much like Buffalo Bill Cody. Because of his long hair, the Indians named him Inuspi. Whatever that may mean is like most Indian names, a mystery.

Brown's background is wrapped up in myth and legend.

Some say that as a child he was a playmate of Edward Seventh and of Her Royal Highness Louise, the Duchess of Argyle. It is known that on December 13, 1857, young Brown was made an ensign of the Eighth Regiment of Foot and transferred to India. From there he went to South America and worked with a pony express outfit. Making his way to the North American continent, he joined General Custer's command and saw the Indian fighting. The story is that he was out riding with dispatches when Custer's forces were wiped out. Brown was a deckhand on Mississippi River boats and he worked his way across the United States to reach San Francisco in 1862. Three years later he turned up in Fort Edmonton. With a companion he made his way through the danger-ridden country of the Blackfeet and the Crees southward to Minnesota where he married a French halfbreed. On his way south he had passed the Pincher Creek and Waterton Lakes district. He narrowly missed being the first white man to see it. That honour went to Lieutenant Thomas Blakiston, a member of Palliser's Expedition, who was there in 1857. It was Blakiston who named Waterton Lakes in honour of Charles Waterton (1783-1865) an English naturalist.

It was something of a coincidence that practically the next white man along, Brown, became the first superintendent of Waterton Park. Today, combined with Glacier Park across the international boundary, Waterton-Glacier International Peace Park perpetuates the long-standing peace between Canada and the United States. Established as such on June 18, 1932, it was the first park to be so dedicated. The 3,200 acre international peace park on the Manitoba-North Dakota boundary was dedicated on July 14, 1932.

Brown became the chief ranger and park warden at Waterton—where a cairn dedicated July 8, 1936, pays him tribute—and he left valuable information behind because, whether he liked it or not, he had to keep a journal. Records of the parks department at Ottawa profited from this in later years and, apparently, judging by the records the department eventually came to agree with Brown that he should have a typewriter. There is a picture of Brown hanging in the

Norlite Building in Ottawa, but there is no suggestion that Brown ever visited the big boss down east. After reaching the position equivalent to park superintendent today, Brown had his hair cut. He then plagued Ottawa with requests. He once asked that he be given more authority to control gambling among the tourists. Knowing something of the background of the countries through which Brown had made his devious ways, and of Brown's background, too, this request was something of a surprise to Ottawa. But they never caught Brown napping in this exchange of correspondence. In 1912, when asked by the parks commissioner to account for a missing fire pail, Brown replied it had been either lost or stolen.

Brown, the man who smacked of Eton and Oxford, was also a man of vision. Among those who settled the west, he was one of the few so gifted. There were one or two leaders, but in the main the west was settled by a lot of little people whose forte was brawn and courage. They learned as they went along. Out on many sub-marginal areas today you happen across clumps of trees or basement excavations. Those sites were as often as not the homes of those who were learning. They learned the hard way and the clumps of trees or basement excavations are their memorials. It was because of what they learned that the very economy of the country progressed and each area found its own niche in that economy.

Brown, of course, had been there long so was a man of foresight backed by experience. In the second Riel Rebellion he was a scout for the Rocky Mountain Rangers. He was a packer for the contractors on C.P.R. construction through the Crowsnest Pass. In the years around the first war he travelled his part of the country pleading with the ranchers to build fences. He could remember the great and hard winter of 1911 when 4,000 cattle drifted into the park area and 2,000 died.

When the girl he married in Minnesota died in 1881, Kootenai Brown buried her on the banks of Lower Lake at Waterton and several years later he married a Cree girl, Nichemoos, and he told Nichemoos that some day airplanes would fly over the mountains. Brown died in 1920, and when some time later the first aircraft from Lethbridge visited the park, Nichemoos, whose death occurred in 1935, was the most excited among the spectators of this big event of that day.

On Brown's cabin shelves were the works of Carlyle, Goldsmith, Tennyson. In his journal, a cultured hand wrote of his requests for more salary—in his days as park official—and of the troubles he had with his employees who thought that if those in Ottawa worked only eight hours a day, so should they.

At times he penned deep thoughts:

To a lady

Oh sister mine by our bright star of birth
Recall the tie that binds us on this earth
Thy friendship's love is all that I dare claim
A wreck upon life's stormy sea without a name.

Brown undoubtedly was one of the first white men to have any inkling of nature's greatness that is now known to lie under the Pincher Creek country. He was an early friend of the Indians. They told him of a substance they rubbed on limbs to cure aches and pains. Brown thought it might be oil. He mixed some molasses and coal oil, gave the Indians a sniff. When they nodded, he told them to lead on. They led him to what became known as Seepage Creek because when Brown punched the sand with his heel up seeped oil. A syndicate did some drilling there years later but nothing of a commercial production was ever undertaken.

But the people of Pincher Creek well know that the place got its start on the ground, not under it. History has it that it got its name when a pair of pincers dropped in the creek by prospectors in 1869 were recovered by a police party in 1874.

The police built a post at Pincher Creek shortly after they opened the barracks at Macleod, but the real reason for moving west about thirty miles was to get lush hay for their mounts. It was that which gave Pincher Creek its start as a farming and ranching community.

The shakedown cruise that followed the arrival of the ship of state in the form of the Mounties was undertaken by an assortment of interesting people. Among them was Francis Willock, who arrived in 1883 with a herd of dairy cows he had driven from steel end at Medicine Hat, a little matter of about 140 miles. Willock, however, made a name for himself and for Pincher Creek in another field. He grew great quantities of rhubarb which he freighted to Lethbridge where the commodity enjoyed a ready sale.

Pincher Creek no longer exports rhubarb, nor does it import polo equipment as did Willock's friend E. M. Wilmot. In 1886 Wilmot brought polo sticks and balls from England. Pincher Creek's residents like to claim it was the first such sporting equipment imported to North America. It was certainly the first in Pincher Creek. The game became quite popular but it has been some time since *The Pincher Creek Echo*—which has a panorama of the Rockies for its masthead —has had a report of such doings. Polo was pretty popular over all southern Alberta in the early days. Even today Calgary has a club.

The brittle files of *The Pincher Creek Echo* tell the story of Pincher Creek, but you can also get it first hand by sitting around the lobby of the King Edward Hotel listening to the old folks. This is a pastime that has been going on for years and had its start in an establishment known as the Bucket of Blood. There are no gory details attached to the name. The place, something of a café became the namesake of an old Old Country pub and those who gathered there were quite serious and generally quite sober about life.

Pincher Creek, as self-contained as it may appear, certainly is not standing still. At Pincher Station, the rail point, you find three grain elevators and plenty of stock cars and therein lies the economic secret of the community. In summer, grain waves far to the east. The year around, cattle that fill the stock cars graze everywhere in all directions, including the highway ditches.

Buyers from everywhere come to Pincher Station when the Community Sales holds its local auctions and money like

$200,000 that may change hands at a single auction is what keeps the town going and growing.

Pincher Creek has progressed a long way from the boyhood days of Fred Shoening. Shoening was born there in 1887. When he was a lad his father would put him on a horse in the morning and he would stay on it out in the open range all day doing his share of the work, and often alone. He had to stay on the horse all day, too. If he ever fell off there was nobody around to put him back on it.

Shoening argues it was adventuresome young men—such as his father, Charles, who came into the area in 1883 after a pack horse trip over the mountains from Walla Walla, Washington, following a long detour through the United States from Ontario—who really opened the country, not the big ranchers. There was not much money around then. If a fellow got $30 for a four-year-old steer he figured he had done pretty well. The ranchers would sell their meat to the butcher in town who would send a man out in the country with a wagon, selling the meat in cuts back to the people who raised it. The ranchers and farmers had no means of storing their own and to a large extent depended upon game.

But as Shoening knew his neighbours, they were ingenious people. He remembers when they made their own plaster. Lime kilns were made by digging a hole twenty feet deep on a hill, at edge of the bank. At foot of the hole, another hole was burrowed in from the side to get in an iron grating. The bottom was then filled with five feet of wood, a fire was started and the hole filled with limestone. The top was left open and the workmen would stay at the site for seven days, continually firing depths of the hole. The limestone, of course, would eventually burn. When flames came out the top the hole was tightly covered to smother the flames and then left to cool. The mass of lime was then shovelled from the bottom and the lumps when dissolved by water were ready for use as plaster.

Shoening is one of those who knew the country before its façade was changed by the fence but he said there was nothing exciting about the transition, except in the movies. The fences came so gradually it was hardly noticed. It was the movies themselves, to Shoening's mind, that changed the country towns, particularly Pincher Creek, quicker than anything else. People then began to drift away from the old-time sociability of the ranch house dance.

Norman Macleod had something to do with that transition locally. When T. H. Hinton remodelled a store into Pincher Creek's first theatre about 1905, Macleod set up a projector, showed two reelers—with sing songs in-between—on a screen of canvas stretched on a frame and kalsomined in flat white so it would not reflect light.

The theatre business in those days had its problems. Because it had a big stage, Pincher Creek's first theatre drew the big stock companies travelling over the Crowsnest line from Lethbridge to Vancouver. Often, said Macleod, they had to be helped on their way. The town's swains would take their girls and a box of candy to see the plays and often it was difficult to distinguish between rustling of the wind around Uncle Tom's Cabin and rustling of the paper around a chocolate tidbit. The problem in Pincher's modern theatre of today is popcorn, as elsewhere. But unlike elsewhere, in Pincher you can get an extra wide seat. The unusual seats scattered through the theatre are a reminder of the old double seats some theatres installed for those who wished to sit close together because they were in love. Or thought they were. But these seats at Pincher Creek are a seat and a half wide, not actually double. They are big enough to give a fat fellow, accustomed to spreading himself on a saddle, a little more comfort. Or to accommodate two thin lovers. And in those seats there is something typical of Pincher Creek itself, the place that never got as big as they thought it would but managed somehow to be different.

You will find the same thing on the big sign the Board of Trade caused to be painted on the side of Jackson Brothers' store (saddlery, men's wear). It is a big map that shows the products and attractions of the district. And it is a far-sighted affair. It lists the Trans-Canada Airlines route, which passes to the north to wing from Calgary to Vancouver but is only within bombing distance of Pincher Creek. It lists the town as on the "main line" of the C.P.R. between Lethbridge and Vancouver. And it lists the Crowsnest Pass route as the Trans-Canada Highway, which was the hope of a great many people not only around Pincher Creek but the district generally. If one is so bold as to point out that there may be a slight error in this setup, that the transcontinental highway will actually pass through Calgary, some solid citizen will answer that it does not matter where they put the highway because the traffic will go over the Crowsnest route anyway. Much of it does, too, for the road forms the southern boundary of a loop through the mountains and also serves Idaho, Washington, British Columbia and way points beyond.

The traffic has changed around Pincher Creek. The buildings have that weather-beaten look of the old west. The streets are a bit crooked and dusty, as they were in the old west. You still hear the clatter of horses but it is a sound mingled with the meshing of gears. The people still come to town wearing sombreros. The Indians still loll in the doorways. But it is not the traffic that Scotty Freebairn, the Pincher poet, heard about, or saw, when he sat around the Bucket of Blood to listen to the shoptalk. It is not the traffic that knew Charcoal, or Op-e-o-wan (Bad Young Man) who was hanged at Macleod in 1908 and of whom Freebairn penned:

It seems a buck called Charcoal
Found another with his squaw,
So he laughed at white man's justice,
And invoked the Indian law.
With a thirty-thirty rifle
He shot him through the head,
And left the squaw ki-yi-ing
For a lover that was dead.

Charcoal not only killed a fellow Blood Indian on his reserve, but in the manhunt that followed also killed a Mountie, Sergeant Wilde. A crafty individual, Charcoal somehow managed to steal the mounts of his pursuers while they were stabled at the ranch of Dicky Bright, who was the son of the famous English doctor and discoverer of Bright's disease. The next time he was sighted, Charcoal was riding an exhausted horse. He was soon overtaken but as Sergeant Wilde, in the lead of the posse, leaned over from his saddle to grab his quarry, Charcoal suddenly wheeled and fired. The Indian then fled on Wilde's horse. Charcoal was pursued into the mountains and back to the plains where he was caught on the Piegan reserve. A tablet to the memory of Sergeant Wilde was erected at the Pincher Creek barracks.

The newcomer to Pincher Creek senses something that leaves him keen and expectant. What he does not see is wrapped up in the memories that break out every year when the Old Timers' Association holds its "do." As if to prove the quality of the age of Pincher Creek, a point is always made of the fact that the association was formed in 1908, which was a mighty young year for old-timers to get together out west.

When the organization was formed the talk was that it should be restricted only to those who had shot an Indian or a buffalo. At the gatherings today, however, the song sheets are likely as not to contain the Red River Valley and the wording of the present song is a contentious matter around Pincher Creek. The old folks call a "garbled radio version" the lines that now read, "remember the Red River Valley and the cowboy who loved you so true"; and, "when you think of the fond heart you're breaking and the pain you are causing to me." They make the seemingly rather sensible comment that in the first place nobody ever heard of an old-time cowboy breaking his heart over a girl, and if one did cause him pain he would be more likely to head for the nearest saloon and get gloriously drunk. Furthermore, they argue that the song so popular out in the west, particularly on so-called western radio shows, actually pre-dated the era of the western cowboy, which was only 1882 or 1883. While it may have been sung by the settlers around Fort Garry, in all probability it was imported from the United States. And, anyway, Pincher Creek's historians will tell you, as if to clinch their argument, the original song was about a man leaving a halfbreed girl, not a girl leaving a man.

In this corner of Canada's cow country there is contentment among the people. And maybe Freebairn caught it when he wrote:

I'm tired of the sights and the city's bright lights,
I long for the peace of the range.
The spell of the mountains, majestic and grand,
The nights that were awesome and strange.

It is still there at Pincher Creek, from the nostalgic noon hour bell that tolls over the town to the beauties of the protective rearguard that is the Rockies.

Only a few miles away on a quiet night in April, 1903, a mountain fell and the motorist today drives over a highway that was blasted from the tumbled rock that buried the village of Frank.

The Frank slide was one of the world's great mountain tragedies. There have been many tragedies in mountain slides, but at Frank an entire section of limestone Turtle Mountain toppled on the sleeping community. Today acres and acres of rock cover the spot and the motorist is literally left breathless as he practically stumbles upon this tragic sight. It may be in keeping with the reverence Canadians hold for such things, but the slide has not been too widely publicized. But the sight of the area today is one of the few in Canada that once a man has seen he would never forget.

Frank was—and still is—a coal mining community. Around turn of the century it was one of the leading towns of the Pass, as the whole area is commonly known. It had a newspaper, *The Frank Sentinel;* hotels, and it was a busy, bustling place that faced on a great wide and beautiful valley locked on the south side by Turtle Mountain.

The miners of Frank worked in the very bowels of Turtle Mountain. They thought nothing of it. If they listened at all it was only with wry smiles to the stories of the Indians. The Indians told of a massacre and of a moving mountain. The massacre has been authenticated and if you consider the Frank slide as a moving mountain, so has the other legend.

The Indians told of how a war party of Blackfeet massacred

a party of Crow Indians at the foot of Turtle Mountain many years ago. This story was more than legend for Big Swan and Crow Chief, two chiefs among the Piegans, who died comparatively recently at the ages of eighty-seven and ninety could tell of the incident. They pointed to Turtle Mountain as the true Crowsnest. It was so named by the Indians because a party of Blackfeet scouts following the Crows who were retreating to the mountains, returned to their main camp to report they had found the "Crow's nest." But to the white man, Crowsnest mountain is a lonely and isolated hunk of rock some miles to the west where ravens roost.

The Indians had another legend about Turtle Mountain. The mountain, before it was shorn on one side, resembled a huge, sleeping turtle. That is why the white men so named it. A pioneer family named Garnett named it in 1881, according to some records. But the Indians claimed in whispers that Turtle Mountain moved. Maybe they referred to harmless slides that occurred during the spring. Or did they? When Turtle Mountain rumbles does it really nod its head? It could be, for there are great fissures at its top today and each year they creep a little wider and a little deeper.

Because of this most of the people have moved from its danger zones. The town of Frank of today is out of any danger from possible future slides. But near Hillcrest, a mining community immediately east of Frank, there are a few families of old people living within Turtle's ominous shadow. They will not move and nobody can force them to. For reasons of their own they will not heed the disaster that befell the people of Frank at 4:10 a.m. on April 29, 1903.

It was a quiet night. There was, for a moment before 4:10 a.m., nothing to distinguish it from any other night. If there was any warning noise, nobody heard it because everybody was asleep in the village. A freight train rumbled eastward around the base of Turtle Mountain and within the mountain the night shift of miners was at work.

Then old Turtle nodded its head.

Within 100 seconds a ledge of limestone 4,000 feet wide and 5,000 feet thick had toppled from a height of 1,300 feet and spewed 70,000,000 tons of rock over two miles of valley, burying 3,200 acres to a depth of 100 feet with great, huge jagged rocks, some as big as houses and small apartment blocks. The portion of Frank that lay in the path of the charge of rock was crushed to a splinter. Its sixty-five sleeping residents may have momentarily awakened, but that was all. The miners within the mountain, its thickness insulating the sound for them, thought another harmless slide had rolled by. When they tried to leave their tunnels as dawn came they found the way was barred. They made their exit through an outlet on the other side and then crept around the mountain to find their homes and beautiful valley had disappeared, and over the whole area lay a terrible choking dust.

Wallace T. Eddy, who lives at Burmis where he is inclined to while away the chilly evenings reading detective stories with his feet in the oven of the kitchen range, remembers that curtain of dust. Burmis is a pretty place where a lumber company provides the industry and a picturesque church a setting much like a Swiss village. It was at one time to have been a railway divisional point. Eddy homesteaded thereabouts in 1884 and he was on his farm, about ten miles from Frank, when Turtle toppled. Eddy said he did not hear a thing that night. But in the morning he was puzzled by the fact that the ground and everything on it, including his cow, was covered with white dust.

The records of the tragedy tell of one survivor—a little girl who is now a married woman at the Pacific coast—and of one hero, a brakeman on the freight train that had just edged its way out of the danger zone. In the blinding dust that turned the night into a fog of white, the brakeman crawled and clambered for more than a mile over the jagged, ripping rocks. He knew not where he was going, for everything that was familiar was obliterated. But he crossed to the other side of the slide and was able to signal the Spokane Flyer, a fast passenger train.

Today and for all time the deathly scene will remain. The highway has been blasted through the rocks. The railway, of course, was rebuilt and for years the Canadian Pacific has been removing rock from Frank for use as ballast on the prairies. It has made no appreciable difference.

Somehow this great pile of rock stands as a symbol of the reverence with which Canadians regard tragedies. If this had happened in some other places, it would not be hard to visualize hunks of the rock, fashioned into ash trays or what have you, being sold as souvenirs. But there is nothing like that around Frank.

Advertising on the rocks is banned—and rightfully so—and there is not even a sign to tell the visitor what it is all about. A sign that was there was knocked down by a truck and never replaced. No doubt this will be eventually remedied. But generally speaking development of anything associated with the tourist industry in the whole Crowsnest Pass area is neglected. There is John Kerr's Turtle Mountain Playground, which offers the visitor facilities for a pleasant stopover within sight of the slide, and elsewhere along the road there are fishing camps, but nothing on a large scale. The people are inclined to blame the government for the lack of publicity, but they do little to further their communities themselves.

Turtle Mountain is visible on a clear day from as far east as Lethbridge. It is like a thing that is alive with one side shorn away. And 7,000 feet up on its head, its hat is a little crooked. Government survey parties make regular checks of tremendous fissures at the top. Each time they find them to be a little wider and a little deeper. Nobody knows, of course, whether another slide will come. And bothered the least are residents of half a dozen cottages between Hillcrest and the base of Turtle.

One of them, Mrs. Artura Brazzoni, told me that in the spring "lots of times rock comes down." She said it goes "whirr" when it comes down. I asked her why she stayed and she just shrugged broad, shawl-covered shoulders. She said she cared for her boys, but not for herself because she was sixty-four and "I'm finished pretty soon."

The slide today has become part of the lives of the people who live amid its remnants. But it still grips their imagination, particularly if they have been away any length of time. And it is sometimes hard to judge the reactions of people. H. Harrison, the C.P.R. agent at Hillcrest for thirty-six years, often smiles over the story the conductor of the mixed train told him one day in 1951. A woman passenger, who had lived at Blairmore, on the west side of the slide, at the time of the slide, was on her way back to that point for a visit. As the train passed the acres of rocks, she looked out the window, turned to the conductor and said, "My goodness, haven't they got that mess cleaned up yet?"

Under that mess of rock lies buried not only Frank's residences, its shops and even a bank, but out in what was the broad, beautiful valley the camp of a construction firm that was about to build a fantastic railway.

The Frank and Grassy Mountain Railway is today just a memory and the town it served, Lille, high in confines of Grassy Mountain, is just a ghost whose pathways are traced by rotting water mains.

When people of Lille came out of the hills they used a narrow, twisting trail or rode the one coach of the Frank and Grassy Mountain Railway which wound over three switchbacks and thirty-two trestles to get where it was going, which from Frank to Lille was only seven miles.

Such costly transportation to develop a comparatively small coal seam was what brought about demise of Lille in 1912, nine years after it was built. Some of the people who then came down for the last time are still living around Blairmore. Some of Lille's buildings, too, are in the mining towns. Some may be seen at Bellevue, adjacent to the highway at the Mohawk Mines. Lille's old mining equipment is still doing service for West Canadian Collieries which built Lille in the first place and which, in turn, grew to be one of the main braces of the Pass.

When Lille was first promoted, it had been planned to make the valley at Frank the site for the coke ovens, burning coal from Lille and Bellevue. As a matter of fact, Frank was destined for big things. A metal company built a plant for the reduction of zinc ores from Slocan, B.C., at Frank, but it never operated. The smelter cost about half a million dollars to build. The ruins are on the northside of the highway just east of Turtle Mountain Playground.

Lille came into being because of gold. In 1901 the late J. J. Fleutot, then associated with Gold Fields of British Columbia, and a company geologist, Raoul Green, went to the area. When coal was found on Grassy Mountain, Fleutot returned to his native France, interested French capital, became vice-president and managing director of West Canadian Collieries and promised that the new coal mining centre would be known at Lille in tribute to the home of the chief shareholders.

The company projected its quaint and fantastic railway from Bellevue, across the valley and then upward to Lille. The line was just started when the construction camp of Pourpore and McVeigh was buried by the Frank slide. The coal firm then decided to build the line from Frank to Lille. Another contracting firm, Brekenridge and Lund took on the job and to overcome elevation difficulties built three switchbacks and crossed and re-crossed Gold Creek with thirty-two trestles to make the seven-mile trip. Brekenridge and Lund owned the first coal mine at Lundbreck, that spot out eastward at entrance to the pass, where you saw the tumbling water falls, and where, if you are at all observant, you may have noticed behind the hotel what could best be described as a masterpiece of prairie architecture. It is what is commonly known on the prairie as an outhouse, but there is nothing like it to be seen anywhere. It is a two-storey, four-compartment affair. The top storey is connected with the second floor of the hotel by a catwalk.

The Frank and Grassy Mountain Railway owned two locomotives, a dozen open cars for hauling slack to the coke ovens which were set up at Lille, a passenger coach which for some reason or other was called Pennsylvania, and a caboose. The grade was so steep a locomotive could take only three empty cars at a time. Once in a while couplings would break and cars run away, but nothing serious happened because the cars simply ran into the banks at the switchbacks.

Lille began operating in 1903. It was strictly a closed, company town. The company owned all the property. Consequently when the town closed, its residents simply packed their personal belongings and moved to other jobs down hill. They took no actual loss. It was a fairly big town. The mine tipple capacity was 1,200 tons in two shifts and the coking plant had fifty ovens. There was a combined boarding house and butcher shop, a happy combination; general store, school, hotel and a liquor store. The latter was run by a former C.P.R. newsagent who had met Mr. Fleutot in his travels and had been persuaded by the financier to move to Lille and get into business for himself.

Generally, the people of Lille made their own fun. Weddings were the big occasions. Everybody would club together and buy great quantities of beer and drink it around bonfires. There was considerable singing. There were many Americans in the area and the national holidays of July 1 and July 4 became marathons. It all ended when the seam became thinner and cost of transportation higher. Lille was dismantled and all that remains are the rotting water mains. But Grassy Mountain's coal is still being worked. It is being stripped on the south side of the mountain, one of the many operations all through the Pass.

Coal is the fuel of industry through the Pass. It has kept the fire boxes of the railways and the home fires burning in western Canada since the railway first came in 1896. The first settlement in the valley proper was Blairmore, named after Hon. A. G. Blair, Toronto, then minister of railways. After a trip over the new line Mr. Blair remarked that at the spot a big town would rise. It was decided to call it Blair. But recipient of the honour said the place he envisioned would be big enough to require more than that in its name. So the "more" was added.

Coal dust trails along the highway and dribbles over the railway ties from town to town in the Pass and the towns are so close together one is never quite sure just when one is left and the other entered. Blairmore's neighbour, Coleman, is only three miles away and its 3,500 residents owe their living to the mines and coke ovens.

Eight miles from Coleman is Sentinel, an apt name for a community at the east end of Crowsnest Mountain which towers 9,138 feet but sits out alone something like a Lonesome Luke. Sprawled before it for three miles is the Crowsnest Lake, a favoured fishing spot where it would never pay to fall out of the boat for the lake is reputed to be bottomless. At any rate, cars that have toppled into it have never been recovered and a story of the valley is that years ago some boxcars of a freight train ran off the track and into the lake and they were never recovered. There is a certain spice added to the story by the report the cars were supposed to be loaded with a shipment of whiskey which by this time—if the story is true—must be as well watered as the lake itself.

Halfway up the lake on the north side, a remarkable spring issues from a large grotto in the face of a limestone cliff and this constitutes the chief feeder of the lake.

A few miles to the west, the nose of the car tips the summit at Crowsnest station at an altitude of 4,449 feet above sea level, one of the lowest passes in the Canadian Rockies. And as you drive over the hump you pass from Alberta into British Columbia but you are still amid the chumminess that marks the entire trip over the Crow as the provincial boundary passes through the town and half of the buildings are in one Province and half in the other.

4

Along the Big Ditch

OF ALL the things which a city could publicize, Lethbridge takes its greatest pride in ditch water.

The city's Chamber of Commerce has turned out expensive brochures under such interesting titles as Dam the Water and Green Acres. As the district acquired more ditch water, the publicists turned out More Green Acres and saw them blossom both in a brochure and a steady land boom.

These brochures are designed to draw to the attention of the rest of the world that this is the Irrigation Capital of Canada, a busy water nymph that every year economically gambols amid more hours of sunshine than any other place in Canada.

Whether it has more wind than any other place in Canada is a debatable point, but it certainly has wind although the Chamber of Commerce is not inclined to blow about it in its brochure. The citizens, however, take this in their stride. If they didn't, they'd be blown over. But they see no reason to hide this oddity about their city and are inclined at times to joke about it, particularly if they can capitalize on the jokes. If you should inquire upon being taken up in a hotel elevator why it moves so slowly, the operator will tell you that it is powered by a windmill and the wind would appear to have dropped. If you should believe this, and the next day find the wind at its height, then take the stairs.

But joke or no, the wind has had something to do with the economy of the big ditch country around Lethbridge. The area's mean annual rainfall, over a period of thirty years, has been 9.96 inches. This moisture condition and the drying influence of the wind was the principal limiting factor in production on dry land farming. That's why Lethbridge is so proud of its ditch water.

On occasion the fact that Lethbridge does have wind will get into the public prints. One such occasion was Sept. 11, 1905, the day before a visit by Earl Grey, then governor-general of Canada. A newspaper report of the day indicated the citizens were having great difficulty getting up the customary bunting and decorations, because of the wind.

When the vice-regal party arrived the following evening the visitors and citizens assembled under a street lamp in front of the railway depot where the secretary-treasurer of the town read an illuminated address. It prompted Earl Grey to say in reply that: "I like your address. It is the most original I have received since I came to the country."

What made it original, probably, was the fact that it was a welcome written in the past tense and out there under the street lamp Earl Grey was told of all the beauties of Lethbridge that he had seen—the night before the day he was taken out to see them.

It seems that things like that have quite often happened to Lethbridge as it has progressed from a place called Ashsoysem to Coal Banks to Lethbridge. Ashsoysem is a Blackfeet Indian word meaning steep bank. Coal Banks is the none-too-original word the white man called the place because he found coal in the banks. As Lethbridge, it stands in memory of William Lethbridge, the first president of the North West Coal and Navigation Company which undertook first development of the district, although the census returns actually go back to some characters who inhabited a nearby place known as Fort Whoop-Up.

Fort Whoop-Up has been described as the first outpost of white man's civilization in Southern Alberta. From its methods of operation, it was probably also the first speakeasy on the continent. It was eight miles south of Lethbridge on the Oldman River and a cairn marks the spot today. In 1867, when Canada was born—and, incidentally, one of the Fathers of Confederation, Sir Alexander Galt, had a great deal to do with development of this area of Southern Alberta —Fort Whoop-Up was doing a big and gay business as the most important trading establishment between Fort Edmonton and the United States border.

It was built in 1867 by two American business men of the day, named Healy and Hamilton, and it was originally known as Fort Hamilton. Healy and Hamilton were inclined to allow happy happenings among the Indian customers and during one of these events, in 1871, there occurred one of those embarrassing things neither the host nor party guests can explain. The fort burned down.

Healy and Hamilton, undoubtedly out of pocket on that deal but still willing to take a chance, re-erected the fort later that year and hung out the old sign, business as usual. And business, as usual, was good. The traders brought their supplies from Fort Benton in Montana, traded for buffalo and other hides with the Indians. Historians are inclined to contend that all this was done in a manner defiant of law and order, but to be fair to Healy and Hamilton enterprise, this was not exactly so. The business was undoubtedly carried on without regard to ethics or good taste, but at the start at least it could hardly defy law and order because law and order, in the uniform of the N.W.M.P., did not arrive on the plains until 1874.

When the Mounties arrived, Fort Hamilton was going strong as Fort Whoop-Up. The business got this happy name which, you must admit, will advertise it for all time, purely by accident. A trader who had returned to Fort Benton from Fort Hamilton was asked how things were going up there and he replied: "Oh, they're still a whoopin' of 'em up." Thus was born, or coined, the name Fort Whoop-Up.

Fort Whoop-Up's business methods were the epitome of simplicity. History has handed down the description of a trader standing at a wicket gate with a tub of whiskey beside him. When an Indian pushed a buffalo robe through the wicket, the trader handed out a tin cup of whiskey in payment. A quart of the concoction would buy a pony. Every day was bargain day and on days when sales were good the grounds around and about were alive with singing, dancing Indians.

When the Mounties hove into sight in 1874 they found Fort Whoop-Up flying the American flag. The only person around the place was an old man who said he was in charge. Healy and Hamilton had fled. The police somehow got in touch with the two traders and offered to buy the fort for $10,000. They needed a fort for themselves and it seemed easier if not cheaper to buy than to build. To Healy and Hamilton it was a seller's market. Always the traders, they figured their new and strong fort was worth $25,000.

There was considerable dickering but Fort Whoop-Up's old factors stuck to their figure. The police considered it too high a price so marched on thirty miles west where they built a place of their own on Oldman River at what became known as Macleod. Fort Whoop-Up gradually fell apart and parts of it blew away and today the site is marked by a cairn on the northeast corner of what is now the Blood Indian Reserve.

In the centre of the City of Lethbridge today, in attractive Galt Gardens, there is a small cannon. It is about three feet in length and is mounted on a broken wooden carriage with wooden wheels. It is a two-pound smooth bore muzzle loader that was cast in 1846 in St. Louis, Missouri. Healy and Hamilton brought the gun to Fort Whoop-Up in 1871. It was acquired by Dave Akers, who had used the fort site for ranch headquarters in later years, and in 1892 Akers sold it to John D. Highinbotam, one of the west's historians, who presented it to the city in 1929.

There sits what remains of Lethbridge's association with those stirring days, the days that started the changes from buffalo hides to boat building to coal mining to the irrigation canals that help raise the sugar beets and the peas and corn to make Lethbridge of today the heart of diversification on the prairies. And within its own boundaries of streets and avenues, with something of the carefree attitude of its pioneers in its veins, Lethbridge today, too, finds diversification in its own amusements.

The city's recreation centre is a showplace. For recreation its citizens are offered everything from badminton (125 members) to curling (500) or, perhaps, golf (600) or tossing horseshoes (30). If you are inclined, there's the Barber Shop Quartette (40 members) the Old-Time Dance Club (400 members) or the Ballet Club (30).

The visitor to Lethbridge today can best enjoy the place by first briefing himself on its history. It is not a city that has preserved a great deal of its past although by parks, place names, tablets it has sought to perpetuate the memories of those who built it and, actually, its very presence is a monument to the far-sightedness of its first citizens. Most prominent among them is the name Galt. To many people in Western Canada, the name Galt is synonymous with coal. Lethbridge is also synonymous with coal and to Lethbridge the name Galt is synonymous with progress.

It was just below the present site of Galt Hospital that the Blackfeet and the Crees, traditional enemies, fought the last great Indian battle in 1870. The Crees lost. They left 250 of their braves on the battlefield. The Blackfeet lost 70 of their warriors. The following summer the Crees sent the Blackfeet gifts of tobacco. As fall was colouring the countryside, the great men of the two tribes smoked the pipe of peace on the banks of the Red Deer River to the north.

That was about the time Nick Sheran was poking around the country. Sheran came up from Fort Benton. He brought along his sister, Marcelia, who was his housekeeper. When Marcelia married Joseph MacFarlane at Fort Whoop-Up in 1877 it was the district's first white marriage. Sheran, in 1872, opened the first coal mine in Alberta on banks of the Oldman River. He was a man of great initiative. He broke his own trails, hauled his coal by ox team for 200 miles to Fort Benton where it found a ready market and founded a vital industry that has contributed greatly to the development of Western Canada.

Today in Galt Park, which years ago was the home port for the bull teams that plodded northward from Fort Benton, there is a cairn to honour Sheran. But it was the Galt family that brought the rapid development to this part of the country. It was the Galts, with their access to British capital, who built the first railways, and who made possible the first irrigation.

From the dreams of those pioneers Lethbridge in 1951 was engaged in a full-scale performance on 360,000 irrigated acres. Two projects in process of completion were to add another 593,000 acres. This makes for stability and higher rural population. On dry land in the west there is an average of 3.5 people per square mile. Where the farmer has the water that he can make work for him, he has smaller farms—averaging a quarter section—so he has many more neighbours, an average of 35 people per square mile.

This phase of development dates to 1879 when Elliott T. Galt, visiting the west to inspect Indian agencies, became interested in Coal Banks' coal outcrops. He interested his father, Sir Alexander Galt, then high commissioner for Canada in London. Sir Alexander interested British capital and in 1881 the North West Coal and Navigation Company was formed with William Lethbridge the president. And that, believe it or not, led to Lethbridge becoming an inland port. It once built boats and barges. It was a business that lasted but a year, although the boats that Lethbridge built served the west well in the Riel Rebellion.

In 1883 the Canadian Pacific Railway was staking its way west, rail by rail and tie by tie, somewhere in the vicinity of Swift Current, Saskatchewan. The railway needed coal. There was coal at Coal Banks. The railway agreed to take the coal at Medicine Hat, about 100 miles east of Lethbridge, but the problem was how to get it there.

Material to build steamers was ordered from Eastern Canada. It was unloaded at Swift Current, moved overland by bull team, some of the heavier stuff to Medicine Hat, the rest to Coal Banks. Skilled shipbuilders were brought from Pittsburgh to Coal Banks via the Missouri River and Fort Benton. By June 1, 1883, they launched the first boat, the *Baroness,* named after Baroness Burdett-Couts, one of the navigation company's financial backers.

The hull was floated down the Belly River to Medicine Hat where the machinery was installed. The *Baroness* was 175 feet long with 31-foot beam. A flat-bottomed craft, it had draught of six inches when empty and twenty-four when loaded. The boat was built of pine, as were sixteen barges that were subsequently made. The pine was obtained from the company's sawmill at Porcupine Hills, sixty miles from Lethbridge. One other boat, the *Alberta,* was built and a third, the *Minnow,* was purchased in Winnipeg. By 1884 there was quite a fleet ready for the Belly. It sailed, but not for long. Looking through old files in Lethbridge, one comes to the conclusion that it was a pretty good idea except it didn't work too well.

What was not taken into account, apparently, was the fact that the boats had to get back to Lethbridge (the name was changed from Coal Banks in 1885) for more coal. The chief period of navigation was during high water and lasted about seven weeks. The trouble was that during high water the current was so strong the boats used as much coal to haul the barges and themselves back upstream as they could carry downstream in the first place. Almost anybody could figure out that such operations would get you nowhere.

But the C.P.R., which would have put the boats out of business, anyway, was quite pleased with the coal. It offered a long term contract if a rail line was built connecting Dunmore Junction, near Medicine Hat, with Lethbridge. In 1885 a narrow gauge railway that became known as the Turkey Trail was built. The North West Coal and Navigation Company received a land grant of 3,840 acres per mile to be paid for at ten cents an acre. In 1889, seeking still more markets, the company, by now known as the Alberta Railway and Coal Company, built another narrow gauge line over virgin prairie to the international boundary, eighty miles south, thence to Great Falls, Montana. This line became the first west of Winnipeg to cross the international boundary. The lines to Medicine Hat and from Lethbridge to the boundary were eventually taken over by the C.P.R. The United States trackage of the southward line was sold to the Great Northern.

The company, by this operation, had acquired something over 1,000,000 acres in land grants. The far-sighted officials knew it would be necessary to supply employment to the people it wanted to open this land. The settlers, obviously, had to live until their lands could produce.

On Lees Creek, to the southwest of Lethbridge at what is now Cardston, a small Mormon settlement had been organized in 1886. These people, a hardy lot led by Charles Ora Card, were well aware of the advantages of irrigation. It had worked for them in Utah. They were trying it on a small scale at Lees Creek.

To the Galts and their associates it seemed logical to unite land settlement with irrigation canal construction. The Dominion government offered its assistance. It seemed natural the settlers of Cardston should introduce the company's representatives to heads of the Mormon Church. C. A. Magrath, a former Dominion surveyor who had joined the company and married a daughter of Sir Alexander Galt, went south to do the honours. The result was an agreement by which the Mormon people would construct the canals, accepting payment half in cash and half in land at $3 per acre. By turn of the century man was making water flow over the farms of the Magrath, Raymond and Stirling districts just as he needed it. As time went on, the areas were settled by peoples of all nations.

That is why, when you travel the highways around Lethbridge today, you meet trucks loaded with coal and trucks loaded with sugar beets and, in season, why you keep running over cobs of corn on the roads. Where, in other parts of Alberta, the travellers see grain trains or stock trains or even trains of tank cars, around Lethbridge in the fall season they see train after train of open cars loaded with sugar beets going to the factories at the place with the picturesque name of Picture Butte, just north of Lethbridge; to Raymond, on the south, or to what could best be described as a giant of a plant built in 1950 at Taber, to the east. The highways are busy with trucks carrying other field products to the canneries.

It is here that ditch water has turned ordinarily unproductive soil into green acres. Here is where man has beaten the drouth. He may have other problems in early frosts, early snows, but he need never sit in his farm kitchen to stare moodily out at the heat waves winging their way over the fields, withering everything in their path.

On these green acres there live people who talk of their sugar beets and potatoes under irrigation averaging twelve tons to the acre, of their corn yielding five tons to the acre, their alfalfa three tons and two crops a year.

There are more green acres to come. Much of what was built by private capital that had a checkered career in the field of delivering water has been taken over by the Government of Canada. The Alberta government, too, is further developing the district with co-operative enterprises, offering assistance in building canals for federal projects.

For the visitor who has an interest in his country, a desire to see what Canada is doing in its own quiet way, a 40-mile trip southwest of Lethbridge is worthwhile. There he comes to the St. Mary River dam. Started in 1946, finished in four years, it is the largest of its kind in Canada, 195 feet high, 2,539 feet wide. It gobbled 4,500,000 yards of material, enough to construct a first class highway 140 miles long. It creates a reservoir with capacity of 320,000 acre feet of water with usable storage of 285,000 acre feet. The water is backed up for seventeen miles and creates a lake six miles wide.

That is only part of the latest development, estimated to cost $30,000,000. Briefly, the project means tapping the Waterton, Belly, St. Mary and Milk Rivers. This will establish beneficial use of Canada's share of four important international streams. The water will be stored in a series of ten natural reservoirs with combined storage capacity of 740,000 acre feet. An acre foot is a foot of water covering an acre. These will be connected by 220 miles of main canals. Another 2,200 miles of smaller canals will be required to move the water to individual farms. It will be 1960 by the time it is completed but beginning in 1951 about 35,000 additional acres were to be served each year and when it is all finished the water will trickle clear to the doorstep of Medicine Hat, at the end of what they used to call the Turkey Trail, the building of which led to settlement that led to irrigation.

Man, in Alberta, has moved slowly but logically.

Lethbridge, however, doesn't live within itself. It is the heart beat, to some extent, of bigger and better farming generally. Its federal experimental station and the science service centre work for the farmer, whether he is on dry land or bending over a ditch, and for the rancher, too, and there are many of the big-hat boys around Lethbridge for much of the area southeast of the city is not suitable for irrigation.

An experimental station is not a particularly exciting place, although the visitor with an interest in plant life of any kind would find pleasure chatting with the men who man the Lethbridge station. These men, and their co-workers in similar stations across the country, are Canada's unsung heroes. It takes great patience to carry on work with plants, knowing the work may or may not pay off in ten years or so. When it does pay off, it puts more money into the pockets of the man on the land, makes the cash registers of the hamlets, towns and cities jingle a merrier tune. But the man in the lab or out on the test plot gets very little out of it beyond satisfaction.

As the Chamber of Commerce points out, Lethbridge is small enough to be friendly yet big enough to have all the amenities that make living pleasant. One of its booklets, while it doesn't give the source of the information, points out that Lethbridge has more autos per 100 population than Alberta or Canada. It quotes the figure of 14.4 per 100 for Lethbridge, against 13.2 for Alberta and 11.1 for Canada. On the same basis, Lethbridge, say its boosters, has more telephones and more radios.

The Lethbridge district is more and more fencing itself in smaller plots, but its people do not have the narrow outlook. The people seem to have inherited something from the early settlers, something that was summed up by Magrath, the man who came west as a surveyor and who became a member of the old North-West Territories government sitting at Regina.

It was many years ago that Magrath referred to the Lethbridge district's "broad-minded visionaries." And in that reference he wrote: "In that unfenced period of the west, one was unconsciously trained, as far as that is practicable, to think of the future as well as the present. In riding across the plains it was always necessary to keep some distant point in view in order that one's course could be maintained, and it was equally necessary to watch the ground over which one was passing in order to avoid badger holes and other pitfalls."

To make a visit to Lethbridge what it should be, one has to appreciate its background. When you do, you even seem to detect a feeling of broadmindedness in the city itself. It could be because it has no tall buildings, that its architecture seems to be of a kind it has adopted for its own: Low and attractive buildings. It could be because of this and its wide streets that you have the impression of plenty of space, plenty of good, clean air to breath and plenty of sunshine. It has more of that than any other place in Canada. One year at the Canadian National Exhibition, visitors were asked to guess what city had the most sunshine. There was a series of buttons before a map of Canada. If the guesser pressed the right button, that city would light up. Lethbridge sat in the shadows until one home-town booster happened along. He pressed the Lethbridge button out of pure patriotism, but when lights flashed and bells rang he was so proud he practically became a fixture at the exhibit.

Lethbridge is one of those cities that gives a man more to think about than to see. It produces both food for thought and food for the table and it couldn't produce anything more important. It is a place that is up front in a parade of the potentialities of Alberta, a Province that is full of potentialities. Its sub-bituminous coal mines in 1951 had estimated reserves of 700,000,000 tons. Its irrigated areas have produced a yearly pack of canned and frozen vegetables with market value of more than $5,000,000. The Lethbridge railway division in a good year has produced 38.9 per cent of Alberta's total wheat production. The feed lot industry has become a major Lethbridge asset. An average of 30,000 cattle and 120,000 lambs have been finished for market on lots in the district. This means an annual income of $9,000,000.

As a dessert to the heavier course of economics one should visit the Gurney Museum, in Galt Gardens, that one-time bull pen now an oasis of trees and lawn in the centre of the city, and also inspect the high level bridge, one of Canada's engineering wonders.

This bridge has been carrying Canadian Pacific Railway trains of the Crowsnest Pass route, and northward to Calgary, over the valley since 1909. It is the longest and highest bridge of its type in the world. It spans the valley in 5,327 feet and when crossing it passengers look down from the dizzying height of 307 feet.

The Gurney museum is enough to make a man dizzy from looking, too. It occupies a complete building in Galt Gardens and is the growth of one man's hobby. In 1936 when Walter Gurney, a salesman, began collecting this and that, he kept the stuff in the basement of his home. His ambition was to make a collection of Canadian animals and birds for their educational value. As the collection grew it also acquired a reputation. Teachers would take classes to the Gurney home to see it. On Sundays so many people would call that Mr. and Mrs. Gurney had to get out for a drive by eight o'clock in the morning or they would not get out all day.

So Gurney approached the Lethbridge city council which gave him use of a former board of trade and tourist bureau building at Galt Gardens. He placed his collection there in 1938. The register by 1951 had reached 92,840 visitors.

Gurney turned from collecting stuffed animals and birds to just about everything. There is a collection of shoes from every nation, shells from all over the world, relics of the war of 1812, and a room full of furniture made of horns from many different animals.

Mr. Gurney has no idea how many thousands of articles are on display on the shelves and in the cases. It was a headache for the insurance company which finally solved its problem by numbering the cases and insuring each case. Now if some way could be found to do the dusting it would cure a headache for Mrs. Gurney who has shared her husband's hobby.

5

From Dinosaurs to Dams

STRETCHING from Calgary to the eastern horizon is the Canadian prairie. It is often called monotonous but it has a beauty of its own. Nowhere else do you see the sunrises and the sunsets that you see on the Canadian prairie. The sky that in the distance seems to meet the land becomes a blaze of colour. On winter nights the sky dances and sparkles with the glory of the Northern Lights. It has that kind of beauty that comes from within a person, not the kind you just stand and stare at. Actually, there is nothing to stare at. You can travel all night and all day to reach Winnipeg from Calgary and in the main you are in the same kind of country.

This is old Indian and Buffalo country. Years ago buffalo by the thousands summered here, their sharp hooves cutting deep into the soil and making trails that can still be seen today on many knolls.

Near Gleichen, sixty miles east of Calgary, there is a cairn in tribute to one of the greatest of the peace-loving prairie Indians. The cairn is less than half a mile from the Trans-Canada Highway and a few miles to the east of it, on top of a high hill, is a grave marked by a tall wooden cross and inscribed, "Father of his people."

That was Crowfoot, great chief of the Blackfoot confederacy, born about 1830 and whose death occurred April

25, 1890. Fearless in war but lover of peace, he promoted unity among the tribes of the plains and friendship with the white man. Under his leadership the Blackfeet ceded to the crown title to their tribal lands in 1877. They remained loyal to the crown during the rebellion of 1885, thanks to Crowfoot's counsel and much to the peace of mind of the settlers of southern Alberta.

Some people refer to the prairie as baldheaded. It may be, but it certainly is not flatheaded. This main street of the west feeds the world with farm produce and the grain elevators that are its landmarks are the skyscrapers of Canada's western Wall Street. Towns have grown around these Lonesome Lukes of lumber. But no matter what may be on each side of the tracks, the elevators are the symbol of the prairie's chief industry and what that industry is in even the smallest of places can easily be learned at a place called Bennett, which ordinarily would be known as a wide spot in the road—if it had a road.

Bennett is a small spot on the map but a big spot in the economy of Canada. Popularly known as a whistle stop, as are so many of its neighbours, it is surprising what it turns out and what the engineers pick up after they whistle.

Bennett has one other building, a red frame shack for the convenience of people who want to board the train. Inside the shack there is a long wooden bench, should it be a long wait, a pot-bellied stove and a box of wood, should it be a cold one, and a big barrel of water, marked "C.P.R. Fire Protection" which would come in handy should one get the stove too warm while waiting.

As Calgary is only sixteen miles away, it is obvious that in this day and age, except in winter, few people would use the lamps or the flags to stop the passenger trains, so the railway looks across the tracks to the big elevator for its business.

In an average year, Bennett will ship 90,000 bushels of wheat worth an average of $1.10 a bushel, taking in all grades, and that is why Bennett is a pretty long block in the street of Canadian finance.

The men who man these elevators that dot the prairie are known as grain buyers and while their days may seem lonely, they are busy. Grain buyers are also grain technicians, public relations counsel and men with a good argument. With their scales they test the grain delivered for weight; with a little gas stove and tubes they test it for moisture content, and if the farmer is not satisfied with his grade, a two-pound sample goes to the nearest grain inspection office and word of the inspector is final.

It is these elevators that pace the traveller as he moves along—there is a saying on the prairie that if it was not for the telephone poles along the road a man would not know he was moving—but a little to the north of the main road that is the Trans-Canada Highway, the visitor drops into a huge, awesome valley that was home of the dinosaurs and it is too bad that Alberta or Canada have not done more about it.

Drumheller, sitting in prehistoric badlands amid unique geological formations, is also the centre of Canada's largest domestic coal field. It is, too, home of a fine agricultural area and one of its neighbours, Rockyford, is the home of a couple of young farmers who have copped world grain prizes. Howard Roppel was only twenty-one in 1951 when he was crowned wheat king at the Toronto Royal Winter Fair, and the year before he was beaten out at the same show for the same title by a neighbour boy, Ricky Sharpe, who was then in his 'teens.

The country in the Red Deer valley, from the tourist viewpoint, is of the championship kind, too, but there is nothing young about it. It is a place where the sharp-eyed visitor can pick up odds and ends of life dating back 60,000,000 years. Some thirty complete dinosaurs have been carted away from the valley in vicinity of Drumheller. So it is more than a shame that Drumheller has no museum of its own.

This country is described as the "graveyard of the dinosaur" but the visitor sees no dinosaurs. He would hardly expect to find them clumping around the hills, scratching their necks on the coal tipples, nor would he expect to be told, after the advertising has enticed him to this place, that the closest one is rattling his bones in the National Museum in Ottawa.

There is no doubt that the badlands of Alberta is the only attraction of its kind in Canada. It is truly a fearsome, frightening place. At one time it was littered with fragments of dinosaur bones and there are still a few around for the patient searcher who wants to get far off the beaten track. But more easily located are pieces of petrified wood, petrified tropical fruits, cones and crystallized shells and juniper wood that can be fashioned into beautiful figurines. The area with its wind-eroded hoodoos and its 500-foot canyon walls that seem to have been gouged out in some battle of ploughing, stumbling prehistoric monsters, is a paradise and a challenge to photographers. The whole valley could well be a national park, something entirely different from the mountains. This suggestion has been heard along its banks from time to time, but nothing has been done about it.

It could be, in the past, that it was a story of Canadians not seeing the forest for the trees. A story told at Drumheller is that the Canadian government did nothing or showed little interest in the dinosaur findings of some years ago until an article in an American magazine brought the Americans on the run and they began shipping bones south.

Canada then acted quickly to take over the collection of what remained of things that lived in the Upper Cretaceous times or toward the close of the age of the reptiles, things that became extinct 60,000,000 years ago. Today their old home in Alberta is a picturesque work nature has jammed deep into the plains and is, as the Drumheller District Chamber of Commerce says, "uncommercialized and unspoiled."

Which is also another way of saying unseen and unknown. But with the coming of the blacktop highway, maybe more tourists will swing from the main line to visit this wild country, tourists apart from the scientists or those for whom such things form a hobby. Just tourists who like to see something that is unusual. And the valley, from Drumheller east to Steveville, is unusual from start to finish.

Back on the mainline there is this place called Bassano. It was named in 1884 by Count de Bassano who would have had no idea that it would in time prosper under slogan of "best in the west by a dam site." It picked up the slogan around 1909 when a dam was built on the Bow River near the town for irrigation. This was the start, under authorship of the C.P.R., of the Eastern Irrigation District, which in 1935 was taken over by the farmers themselves.

Bassano, while it has the dam and the slogan, got little of the irrigation because of the lay of the land. The water went to work farther east and the forward-looking individuals of Bassano who promoted a street car line out to the dam because they thought it would be southern Alberta's biggest resort, or something, quietly dropped the idea.

Bassano is still busy. It booms with cowboys, oil workers and farmers on a Saturday night. It lives up to the traditions of its ranching days. The dress of the young men consists of a cowboy hat, bright shirt and blue denims. High heeled boots click on the sidewalks. But the noises that are heard as the people depart for the range and the farm are those of whirring car starters, not the clump of horses' hoofs.

Over in the beverage room of the Imperial Hotel there is a table that bears the scars of other days. None of the old-timers like W. J. Caldwell, Stoney Roberts and Roy Lane—old range hands who today are a trio known hereabouts as the Stoney-Lane outfit—can rightly remember just when it was that the cowhands started carving the brands on the table. All they can remember is that the cowboys would get together and get to drinking and carving and they must have done a lot of carving for the table top today is a solid mass of 200 different brands of outfits from all over Alberta.

I went down to see this table with Caldwell and Roberts, after waiting while Caldwell dug up a clean, fresh shirt and Roberts dusted off his battered hat. Caldwell was 77 and Roberts 75 and with Lane they rated among the oldest of the men of the range of southern Alberta. But there was still plenty of life in the party, and the others had been raw-hiding Caldwell for days for having kissed a girl at a big community supper.

Towns were as scarce as girls when these fellows first hit the country. There were no fences and cattle roamed from Medicine Hat to Bassano and the men who kept them in check were out on the range from April to December. These men talked of roundups of 30,000 head and to settle this or that argument they referred to a well-thumbed Saskatchewan-Alberta brand book of 1907. Roberts, who had come out from New Brunswick in 1893, had been a cook. The "guy who piloted the wagon" and the night hawk—who took care of 125 saddle horses at night—helped him to make the two moves a day. About once a month he would hit a town and load up with supplies to fashion the flapjacks and the pies that were two inches thick.

Just, as in retirement, these happy souls did not seem to worry about directions as to where they were going from here in, they had no worries in the days when there were no roads, when the country was nothing but a sea of grass and the rivers and buttes formed the landmarks that made the maps. It was Caldwell who remembered coming up from Idaho in 1902 with a pack outfit of 160 horses, and of how he moved from Lethbridge to Blackfoot Crossing, about 125 miles, and saw only one man the whole way.

In 1906 Caldwell had 409 cattle and the next spring, after the roughest winter the country has experienced, he had 99 and he guessed Lane could remember his father's losses, down on the Bar-U of High River fame.

"Bad," said Lane, a man of few words.

That is why the gnarled fingers seemed to move over the grooves of that battered table with the fondness a person may unconsciously express in dusting a picture of a loved one. And when they got back to their outfit, a trim little home on the west side of town, they figured those had been pretty good days when everybody was your friend and you just stayed where you stopped and if your horse was tired they would give you another.

It was the coming of the farmer with his fence, and the dam with its water that changed all that and made Bassano into a community where they both farm and ranch and in their spare time do a spot of fishing.

Brooks, a pretty town just forty miles to the east, received the benefits of Bassano's dam. There are so many trees around Brooks today that the visitor would think he is in a park belt. But every tree within forty miles was planted since the irrigation waters came in the First Great War years. And the people have no intention of laying down on the job. The irrigation water is ever moving farther afield and when a man takes a new farm he is required by his contract to plant a certain number of trees.

At the Alberta Horticultural Station in Brooks blossom time is something like it is in an Okanagan Valley community in British Columbia. The irrigation water transformed what was a piece of flat, barren land into Lake Newell, about twelve miles long and four miles wide. It had a high spot that the Brooks Kinsmen club converted into an island and named Kinbrook. A causeway leads the visitor to its twelve acres of unexpected beauty.

Lake Newell gives the anglers for miles around their summer fun with the pike and pickerel. In the winter it is thrown open for a period of commercial fishing for whitefish and during that period the night train to Calgary is always half an hour late leaving Brooks because so much fish is loaded. Every summer pelicans and cormorants, birds that before were total strangers to this neck of the woods, soar over Newell's waters and their breeding ground–goodness knows how they discovered it–is known locally as Pelican Island, a place that some day may lead to a modest fertilizer business.

The waters go on to feed the otherwise dry land, irrigating about 100 acres out of every quarter section, and the mile-long concrete viaduct which carries the water over a stretch of flat country was at one time considered to be one of the engineering wonders of the whole country. Today, the long flume on a series of stilts, is a strange sight out on the prairie.

Irrigation has been the medicine for this area that Captain Palliser, a travelling man for the Colonial Office back in 1857-1860, reported as being unsuited for settlement. Now Medicine Hat, that fortunate city which Kipling early in the century described as having "all hell for a basement" because of its gas fields, is hopeful of getting in on irrigation.

There have been some small, private projects around "The Hat" by those living adjacent to the South Saskatchewan River, which flows through the city and on occasion in the spring makes a nuisance of itself. With further development of irrigation eastward from the green acres of the Lethbridge belt, because of the St. Mary-Milk River development, and because of the Bow River development on an old Canada Land Company project, water that wants to work will soon flow to Medicine Hat's back door.

Medicine Hat, the first city in Alberta on the Trans-Canada Highway's eastern leg within the Province, was founded on an abundance of gas. For many years it was cheaper to let the street gas lights burn all day than to hire a man to go around turning them off and on, a noteworthy fact that made Robert L. Ripley's "Believe It or Not" column, but which is now outdated because the street lighting is electrical.

But the gas, along with valuable seams of lignite coal, has made Medicine Hat, along with its neighbour of Redcliff—which sits on red cliffs—into such a manufacturing centre that it has for one of its slogans, "gas made our town into a city." It is also known as "the gas city of the west," but most people call it "The Hat," and their friends know what they are talking about.

The gas that has developed The Hat area's $35,000,000 yearly production that includes brick and tile, linseed oil products, pottery, sewer pipes, glassware, was discovered by accident. In 1883 the C.P.R. was drilling for water at nearby

Carlstadt (now Alderson) when a gas pocket was struck. It ignited and burned down the drilling rig. Nobody got terribly excited about it, except the people who owned the rig and the section workers who had gas to heat their homes. In 1891 far-sighted Sir William Van Horne, the C.P.R. president, offered the town use of a drilling outfit if it would look for gas. Gas was found at 600 feet, although its depth today is 1,000. First industrial use of it was made by Charles Colter, a plasterer. Colter burned his own limestone, which was picked up on the prairie. He conceived the idea of digging a pit, filling it with limestone and piping the gas to the bottom of the pit.

In 1899, when the town was incorporated, the council retained the gas as a public utility, establishing a precedent in Alberta by being the first to own and operate its own light, heat and power services. The city has made no attempt to charge high rates and this coupled with the abundance of gas has drawn industries to Medicine Hat like a magnet. Gas is sold so cheaply for industrial use that the cost is the equivalent of coal at 57 cents a ton.

On occasion the eyes of the country have turned to Medicine Hat for other reasons. Many years ago it was the most northerly weather station. Because of this it became known as the place "where the weather comes from." It was not bad publicity except for the fact people everywhere else made the remark only when the weather in their community was cold. Medicine Hat has since gone to great pains to point out that its mean summer temperature is 62 and its mean winter temperature is 42.5—both above zero. It has quietly succeeded in killing the popular conception that everybody in Medicine Hat wore buffalo coats and got around on snowshoes.

Then it became known as the place where Hatfield, the Rainmaker, enjoyed such success. In 1921 the farmers, who have never been bountifully blessed by nature in the way of moisture from the skies (the area has one of the longest frost-free periods in the west, but lack of rain and the drying winds in summer are hard to beat) imported Mr. Hatfield from the United States. The day he arrived he was given a luncheon at a hotel and in return for such a welcome, not to mention the $8,000 he was to receive by public subscription, he promised rain.

Hatfield, with two wagon loads of equipment and a great crowd of people in tow, was taken 20 miles out to Chappice Lake. He set up a tower on a high hill, several trays were elevated on the structure and wires were dropped from the trays to the earth. The trays were supposed to contain chemicals from which fumes would rise and condense moisture in the clouds and cause rain over a radius of 100 miles.

Well, rain came. The jubilant ones blessed Hatfield. But it kept on raining. Then everybody blessed Hatfield. The land was soaked and the people pleaded with him to shut the thing off. One farmer suggested it would be better if he could arrange for a light shower every three days and preferably at night. It stopped raining four days later, then the dry winds came and the situation was the same as usual. The farmers demanded action. Hatfield said the clouds were too high for his fumes to reach them. One joker in the crowd said they were just empties going back. Hatfield promised rain within a week but it failed to come, so he accepted $5,500 for the 4.24 inches of moisture that had fallen and then he quietly left.

More recently the community has been in the news because of its river serpent. This long and knobby citizen of the deepest parts of the South Saskatchewan is supposed to come up now and again, shake himself then sneak up on a bank and snare a sheep or a calf for lunch. There are people who claim they have seen it lolling around at mid-river on a warm day. Nobody has made claim to seeing it sneaking up on some unwary farm stock, although farmers have reported stock has mysteriously disappeared. This, it seems, generally happens when somebody figures Medicine Hat is slipping in the news of the day. Two and two, on such occasions, are put together and the serpent gets the blame, although it possibly should be mentioned that the party who did the original adding was a newspaperman who otherwise lives a quiet and respectable life.

In 1951 the city received considerable publicity, including numerous trans-Atlantic telephone calls from Old Country newspapers, by having an English girl sit on a pole for a week, most of it in wind and rain, to advertise the city's rodeo. Two firemen were hurt when a ladder slipped while they were taking the lady something to eat. She lived on a canvas-covered platform on top of the pole, listened to the radio, had a special telephone to receive calls, and for exercise would appear every once in a while and do a little dance and wave to the crowd below.

Flushed with the success of such things, the Chamber of Commerce, its members made weary by a tiring winter, no doubt, advertised the next spring for the purchase of an ogopogo egg on which it was willing to pay the freight from anywhere in the country. They did not say what they were going to do with it.

Medicine Hat is also the home of Mrs. Walter Ratcliffe. Where most people go down to the river to bathe, or to fish, Mrs. Ratcliffe goes down to bait rattlesnakes. Because of this, she has become known locally by the rather tactless nickname of "the snake woman." Mrs. Ratcliffe is a tall, slim and pleasant woman and with her what at one time was a hobby has become a business—that of supplying Canadian circuses with snakes—and her partner is her son, Buckley. He is a husky, well-manicured and mannered young chap who wears a snakeskin doo-dad in his lapel and on occasion sports a snakeskin tie.

When I visited with Mrs. Ratcliffe she was nursing a thumb that looked as if it had been boiled. She said, quite casually, "A snake did it." In her dusting she moved from one table to another a jar that contained a snake, something of a pet.

Mrs. Ratcliffe had been bitten while out snake hunting.

To fight the effects she had slashed her arm at points up to the shoulder and put suction cups on it to draw out the poisons. Snake hunting is a little more dangerous in this country than in the United States where the business is more organized and more anti-toxins are available.

Mrs. Ratcliffe thinks snakes are tidy and clean things. They seldom harm anybody unless they are frightened or angered and actually perform useful service in killing insects and gophers that cause losses to the farmers.

The Ratcliffes do their hunting amid the rocks and cliffs near the river. Apparently there are trade secrets among snake hunters and Mrs. Ratcliffe was reticent to explain just how she and Buckley go about their business. Their chief implement, it would seem, is a stick about the length of a broom handle. It has a wire hook on one end. The hook is slipped over the snake and the rascal fastened tight by pulling on the wire at the safe end of the stick. The snakes are carried home in covered pails and kept in sunken pits. Some become live circus attractions; the skins of less fortunate ones become wallets, belt and even ties. The ties have cloth backing and for the fastidious, the knot is already tied. It fastens around the neck by elastic.

There is an art to catching snakes and judging by the products hanging in Mrs. Ratcliffe's home, there is also an art to giving the things a good tanning once they are caught. But what this is, she was keeping to herself. As Mrs. Ratcliffe said, give a business too much publicity and—you can take her word for this—it gets overcrowded.

Snakes and serpents are wrapped up in the very history of the name Medicine Hat. The origin is somewhat obscure and reputable historians, such as members of the Geographic Board of Canada and J. P. Turner, historian of the Royal Canadian Mounted Police, have uncovered numerous stories.

One is that Medicine Hat is a translation of the Blackfoot Indian word "saamis," meaning headdress of a medicine man. Another explanation connects the name with a fight between the Cree and Blackfeet tribes when the Cree medicine man lost his bonnet in the river. Another connects it with the slaughter of a party of white settlers and the appropriation by an Indian medicine man of a fancy hat worn by one of the victims. Still another explanation is that the name applied originally to a hill near the city which resembled a hat. This hill, incidentally, was styled Medicine Hat on a map of the Department of the Interior in 1883. Still another story concerns the rescue of a squaw from the South Saskatchewan River by an Indian brave upon whose head a medicine man placed his hat as a token of admiration and, possibly, appreciation.

The most fantastic and the one, of course, to which the city gives the greatest publicity, concerns an Indian legend. It makes good reading in the guide books if for no other reason than to make people go down and stare at the river: It was this story, too, which was vouched for by most Indians interviewed by Mr. Turner on the subject in 1905.

The legend is that a Blackfeet warrior had a vision while camped on the river. Ice covered the river but there was a small patch of open water caused by the current. A figure appeared from this opening. Some versions say it was the figure of an Indian chief, others that it was a huge serpent. Whatever it was, it was wearing an elaborate headdress adorned with eagle plumes that undoubtedly were a little wet if not frozen stiff. It seems that the warrior who enjoyed this dream was courting the maiden of his heart at the time and he was told by the object that arose from the river, eagle plumes and all, that if he threw his loved one to the underwater creature he would become the greatest war chief of all his tribe. The girl agreed to this and was tossed into the water and the place became known as the "spot of the Medicine Hat."

Whatever the origin, Medicine Hat is as interesting as its name. It covers 9,600 acres of river flats and hillside along the river. With irrigation water gradually coming closer, it is looking for many more new citizens to share its beauties in the next decade.

They have made a lot out of the site that was first occupied by the tents of those who came with the railway survey, including the coloured woman from the United States who started a laundry business and contended she was the first "white woman" in the country.

She was once arrested for some misdemeanour or other and this occurrence she described as a fine inducement for settlers. Maybe The Hat has kept that in mind. Today it makes everybody welcome and the visitor who takes a parking ticket over to the police station will receive pleasant conversation and lenient treatment from the station sergeant, whether or not he is a member of the Chamber of Commerce.

6
The Cowtown

THE best way to look over Calgary is from the higher level of the highways coming from the north, south or east because from them you see the full city in the beautiful valley of the Bow and the long line of the Rockies rising like a painted backdrop to the west.

Beneath you is one of the youngest cities in Canada and at the same time one of the continent's best known, simply because for one week each year its citizens let down their hair, engage in a range country wing-ding known as the Calgary Stampede, something an American travel editor described as not an event but a state of mind.

What Calgary has grown to become it owes to people with an adventuresome spirit—the same spirit that makes little boys want to be cowboys—and what it has for a city site it owes to the Mounted Police who decided in 1875 that this was a right smart place to build a post.

The first police detachment was commanded by Inspector Brisebois who issued an order that public documents sent out must be headed Fort Brisebois. The next year Colonel Macleod took command and it was he who suggested the name Calgary. In the Scottish tongue, of which Macleod was no doubt familiar, this means clear, running water. Macleod probably had the Bow River in mind, but he may also have had a personal reason for his family home was Calgary, a small estate on the Isle of Mull in Scotland.

It is, however, an apt name for a city on the clear-running Bow that is sometimes green and sometimes blue and which in turn derives its name from the fact that the Indians found that the fir trees along its banks made excellent bows. The city's second river joins the Bow at an angle of an elbow and hence is known as the Elbow.

With the Mounties came the first trading companies—the I.G. Baker outfit, of Montreal interests, and the Hudson's Bay Company. The residents were dependent mostly upon the old trail to Macleod and thence to Fort Benton, Montana. Trading was a tricky business. A Calgarian of today who took part in it is Ernie King, who has become something of an unofficial weather bureau for the citizens. When King appears in his white flannels the citizens figure summer is here and they get out the garden hose. When King takes off his summer suit the newspapers dutifully make mention of this and everybody starts cleaning the storm windows.

It was King, incidentally, who introduced the bowler hat to the Kootenay country of British Columbia when he was running a gents' clothing store at Kaslo. People went to Kaslo from as far as Nelson to buy his derbies. The prospectors of that day, in the nineties, were gentlemen well dressed in silk shirts and bowler hats, thanks to King. King has worn a derby—in summer he sports a boater—since he was ten years of age and he says there is no hat like it. It is, apparently, a wonderful headpiece in a high wind and that also serves to introduce the fact that on occasion Calgary has high wind of which the Chamber of Commerce as a rule is strangely quiet.

In his trading days, King would go to one point in the community to trade with the Blackfoot Indians and to another to trade with the Sarcees. There was, the authorities figured, no sense in inviting trouble by having the Indians together at the same place at the same time.

The Indians then favoured blankets made in the Old Country. The blankets were designated by stripes as from one and a half to four points. Each point represented a dollar to the Indians as a medium of exchange and also indicated the size of the blanket. The blankets of one and a half to two and a half points were for the papooses. Those from three to four points were for adults. The braves liked those in plain shades, the squaws liked them striped and the papooses were not fussy. The Indians were good traders and quick to learn. If one got a blanket worth a dollar less than the number of points there was a regular pow wow about it. What are advertised as point blankets are still a popular commodity of trade among tourists today, particularly those from the United States, but of course the medium of exchange is a little different.

When the railway arrived in 1883, Calgary had a population of 500. The following year it was incorporated as a town. It was the railway, coupled with a Dominion government land grazing policy and the fact that there was developing an influx of range cattle from over-grazed lands of the United States, that gave the first leg-up to Calgary, which was incorporated as a city in 1893, a mere eight years after its town council had settled the business of hiring a night watchman.

The grazing policy and influx of range cattle developed the tremendous ranching industry. The railway, which was most anxious to keep blood flowing in its own arteries, used land it had acquired by government grant to begin development of the farming economy. Much of the area, however, had insufficient rainfall so to hasten the payoff the railway introduced an irrigation scheme on some 3,000,000 acres to the south and east of Calgary. By 1902 the city was headquarters of the largest irrigation project on the continent, a fact which in 1914 led it to being host to people from all over the globe at an international irrigation conference. That was the same year that Calgary unveiled its monument to South African War veterans and began recruiting for another war.

That year, too, Turner Valley blossomed in Calgary's back door to the south and Calgary became the hub of the oil industry. Oil companies bloomed all over the city and to emphasize a point people waved blocks of shares at each other. Oil today is farther afield, but the business office, for at least 500 oil companies, is Calgary which in 1950 was the sixth city in Canada in amount of cheques cashed. Oil today is drawing the bulk of Alberta's publicity, but Calgary, like most of the Province, knows its foundation is still in agriculture and ranching and its leading newspaper, *The Herald,* runs a daily column under the heading of "Agricultural Alberta."

The ranching development drew young men of adventure. Strangely, this same strain, was still inherent in young men of both the range and the farms during the last war. The Royal Canadian Navy was surprised to find that those accustomed to the saddle or the tractor seat, and who had never seen the sea, made fine sailors.

Calgary cherishes its nickname of cowtown. It came by it of good parents, it is true, but it realizes, too, that it is worth millions in advertising today. If Calgary as a cowtown in its growing days was not exactly as pictured in the movies, what is the difference? At one time it had twenty-one saloons and because they were actually against the territorial laws, they operated as soft drink parlours. The town draymen were kept busy hauling what the bills of lading termed barrels of coal oil from the railway station to these various soft drink places. Everybody knew that what was in the barrels gave a different glow than coal oil, but nobody ever traced them to Winnipeg to find out who it was that sprinkled coal oil on the outside of the barrels in the first place. The effect served its purpose and it was best to leave well enough alone.

When the government in its wisdom rectified this situation and stopped making criminals out of thirsty men, there was quite a rush to get into the bar business. One fellow started with a bar twenty-five feet long and a free lunch room, but as it is when the market is flooded, beer dropped from a quarter for a schooner to two schooners for a quarter, the new business men found all was not smooth sailing and gradually the thing levelled off to a sober business.

Those were the days that brought to Calgary men who were to become among Canada's best known citizens. Pat Burns was a young man of thirty-four, fresh from Ontario, when he set up a slaughter house in 1890 and laid the foundation for Canada's biggest meat packing business. In 1931, when he was seventy-five the country honoured him with a senatorship.

A struggling young lawyer hung out a shingle and the name on it was R. B. Bennett. Still told with relish are stories of Bennett's long feud with an early newspaperman, Bob Edwards, of Calgary and High River *Eye-Opener* fame who wrote of things as he saw them, or sometimes, as he thought he saw them. The C.P.R. in those days was bothered quite frequently with wrecks. Each of these got great prominence in Edwards' paper. Bennett, representing the railway, took up the matter with Edwards who promised to lay off. The next issue had a heading in big type, "another C.P.R. wreck" and under the heading was a picture of Bennett. The voters of Calgary, however, laid out the stepping stone for a career that led Mr. Bennett to the Canadian prime ministership and in retirement in England as Viscount Bennett.

Bennett and Burns and others will live forever in the big hearts of the people of the range, and tucked away in those same hearts there is appreciation, too, for the men like Edwards who in their own way were quite brilliant and who brought many smiles to lighten the days of hard sledding.

The days of cowboys riding in the streets have long since passed, but Calgarians show an extreme fondness for riding horses and the white Stetson which the city itself or its numerous organizations give away by the dozen to distinguished visitors each year, has become a Calgary trademark.

Naturally, then, the city's big show each year is a page from the old west. The Calgary Stampede is the biggest outdoor show of its kind in the world. And Stampede Week (it is always capitalized in Calgary) is no Week for the cynic. Business leaders and clerks go to work attired in western costume. The whole town lets down its hair and the main street, Eighth Avenue, is one long square dance every morning. Indians ride back and forth in their colourful trappings. Chuckwagons at every corner serve flapjacks and bacon to thousands without charge and people who are late for work never

Mormon Temple at Cardston

Famous White-faced Cattle in Corral of Bar-U Ranch at High River

Indian Cemetery and Memorial Cross on Blood Reserve between Macleod and Cardston

The St. Mary Dam, South of Lethbridge

The City of Calgary

The Town of Bellevue and the Frank Slide in the Crowsnest Area

Chuck Wagon Race, The Calgary Stampede

Indian Parade, The Calgary Stampede

Business Street in Lethbridge

An Irrigated Crop in the Lethbridge District

BADLANDS EAST OF DRUMHELLER

DAM ON THE BOW RIVER AT BASSANO

Drumheller

Medicine Hat

A Double Harvest in the Wizard Lake
Oil Field near Edmonton

City of Edmonton

Logger and Sawmill at Winfield

ELEVATORS AT SEXSMITH IN THE PEACE RIVER COUNTRY

GRAVE OF TWELVE FOOT DAVIS OVERLOOKING THE VALLEY WHERE THE PEACE AND SMOKY RIVERS JOIN

Mount Rundle and the Vermilion Lakes

Banff Springs Hotel, Banff

Mount Eisenhower, Formerly Castle Mountain

Lake Louise and Victoria Glacier

Bears on Golf Course at Jasper Park Lodge

Mountain Sheep near Banff

Tourists at the Columbia Ice Fields

Fording the Smoky River in Jasper National Park

View of the Canadian Rockies

Jasper

Cameron Falls in Waterton National Park

worry about missing breakfast. Everybody is your neighbour, whether from the next street, next Province or the next state.

Downtown Calgary in The Week is full of the sounds of people having fun, the sounds of guitars and accordions, of people singing and calling off the squares and clapping hands and shouting yippee—much to the surprise of first-time visitors who arrive by train and are taken to their hotels in horse-drawn vehicles.

Why do the people do this? Why do they come from miles around to play tunes and flip flapjacks? Why do people who otherwise dress the same as people anywhere else, appear in western pants and bright shirts and big hats? Why do people from neighbouring towns leave their businesses and come in to Calgary for a week of such shenanigans? A man who was doing it tried to explain it to me in this way: "We get a lot of fun out of it and we are neighbours. Calgary often does things for us so we come in to help it out." He amplified what the American travel editor had said, because neighbourliness is only a state of mind.

That is why Calgary's Stampede has become such a success. It is the reason most community things in Calgary are a success, except, possibly the business of cleaning the streets. It has the dustiest streets in the country. But so far as a show is concerned, Calgarians usually see that it is by the people more than for the people. It takes a long time to get something to that point, such as the Stampede, just as it takes a long time to get to know your neighbours well enough to drop in at any time in your carpet slippers and dressing gown and with your hair down. When that point is reached, a city, as a neighbourhood, has its own personality. Calgary has that personality the year around.

What goes on at the fair grounds during Stampede Week is something else again. It has come a long way since 1912 when George Lane, Pat Burns, A. E. Cross and Archie McLean backed the first big show. It was then an agricultural fair and a gathering for local cowboys. It now draws up to 400,000 for the week.

The cash customers are really honouring the rancher and the horse—not to mention the farmer—because the rodeo is one of the few sports to develop from an industry. Today it is a third-ranking sport on the continent and is listed among fun and games at some universities. This Western sport has become just as popular in mining towns in the mountains as in the stock town; as popular in the small town as in a city, even blasé New York. It began with the competitions among men who went from one ranch spread to another. It has been much the same throughout the years except for the chuck-wagon racing and the fact that all events have become professionalized on an international level. The contestants have changed, too. In the fall when cowboys gather in Calgary for their Alberta circuit awards they always have their photos taken while wearing cowboy hats. Otherwise most of them look like insurance salesmen.

Chuckwagon racing, the big thrill of the Calgary show each evening, is fast becoming something peculiar to Alberta. Nobody knows the reason for this. Chuckwagon racing originated in the early ranching days and Guy Weadick, one of the originals of the Calgary Stampede and the man credited with originating the term itself, is the chap to tell you how it got to be run under the rules of today.

There was a time when the wagons raced from a standing start, rolled around the track and into the enclosure. The stoves would be unloaded and a fire started and the first outfit to show smoke was the winner. This was stopped when some bright boys got chemicals from the drug store and made smoke in no time.

The procedure was then reversed. The wagons hit the track after circling barrels in the enclosure. They start as the stoves are being loaded. They go around the barrels to equalize the distance they travel before reaching the race track. After circling the track, with outriders yelling alongside, they wind up under a finish line.

Calgary is not a place to visit for its historical background. Actually, it has none. It makes no pretence to having any, either. Such explorers as Thompson, Palliser and such missionaries as Rundle, McDougall and Lacombe are associated in one way or another with the foothills, but not the birth of Calgary itself. Rev. John McDougall, who is remembered best for his work among the Stoney Indians of Morley, west of Calgary, preached for two years in a trader's store before building a church in 1877. The trader was good enough to close the store for these services. The first church in Calgary was established by Rev. Constantin Scollen, OME, an Irish priest. He opened the Mission of Our Lady of Peace in 1875.

So rather than a family tree, Calgary has a heritage. And it has many branches. One is the friendliness of its people. You notice it on the streets or in the shops and you can read it out loud on a sign at the gateway to a big dairy farm near the city. The sign invites the visitor to drop in as "the latch string is always out." It is a saying and an invitation that goes back to pioneer days when doors had inside latches which were opened by a string run through a hole.

For a young city Calgary is setting its own pace in the arts. Its Allied Arts Centre—or Coste House—a twenty-eight-room mansion, offers everything from an art gallery to instruction in ceramics and from the ballet to a model railway on the top floor. Thirty groups participate in its activities. It is financed by private donations with the city contributing $3,500 and the Province $500 a year. In the summer, Bowness Amusement Park, operated by the transit system which started it to drum up business when a ten-mile street car ride was a regular journey, draws citizens to its eighty acres of playground and lagoon adjoining the Bow River for boating, swimming, dancing, picnics or just lounging.

At the east end of the city, on St. George's Island, the Calgary Zoological Society and the city parks department operate a zoological garden with attractions that range from a polar bear to wolves, coyotes, an African lion, Arctic fox and numerous birds. It was started from a single specimen, a black tail coast deer donated by a midway show in 1922. The gardens certainly have some of the biggest attractions in town. It is the only park in America with life-sized models in cement and concrete (thirty of them) of dinosaurs, and there are two houses of fossilized remains.

When the first through train reached Calgary in 1886—from Montreal *en route* to the Pacific Coast—among the passengers were Sir John and Lady Macdonald and George Pickering. Mr. Pickering, who was three years of age at the time, may be found today out in the Inglewood Bird Sanctuary, where the Bow and Elbow flow together on Calgary's east side. The sanctuary is on the Colonel James Walker estate and Mr. Pickering has seen it develop from fifteen mallards that dropped in in 1929, to some 400 acres and 6,000 birds today. It is advertised as an attraction for visitors, but Mr. Pickering is quite disappointed by this. He says the visitors are usually disappointed, too. It is true the sanctuary has 6,000 birds . . . but they are there in the winter, not summer. For the nature lover, however, a chat with Mr. Pickering is worthwhile. He is coming to the conclusion that western Canada is developing a stronger breed of bird because of so many successive late hatching seasons. The birds do not develop wing power to fly south for the winter and their offspring as a result are gradually becoming more hardy.

Another tradition of Calgarians may be helping these stay-at-homes, just as it is appreciated by the citizens. This is the chinook, the warm wind that drifts over the mountains from the Pacific. Chinooks are preceded by a picturesque arch which causes people on the street to start undoing their overcoats button by button. The chinook can lift the temperature by fifty degrees in three hours. It does not melt the snow as much as it seems to absorb it. Calgarians, too, are well treated in the matter of sunshine. In an average year the sun beams brightly but not always warmly for 2,222 hours.

The chinook is the subject of many fascinating stories around Calgary. The best concerns the chap who was driving a sleigh in from the west when a chinook appeared behind him, rapidly melting the snow. The fellow spurred his horses and as he raced into the city the front runners were on the snow but the back runners were creating what was described as "a helluva dust storm."

7

The Calgary-Edmonton Trail

THERE is one thing to be said for the Alaska Highway: It has certainly added class to the old Calgary-Edmonton Trail.

When you are leaving Calgary, headed north, and come to the intersection of 16th Avenue N.E., and 3rd Street N.E.,—and if you think that's confusing wait until you get to Edmonton, home of the astronomical street numbers—take a look at the sign posts.

One, among a series at important intersections to guide the wayfarer through Calgary's streets, indicates that up this way in quick succession are: Edmonton, Sunset Drive-In Theatre, Airport, Alaska. The other, placed by the Alberta Motor Association, which does a good job of marking Alberta's highways, indicates that straight ahead is Edmonton, 191 miles, and the Alaska highway.

Actually, the Alaska Highway's mile zero begins at Dawson Creek, B.C., in the Peace River block, 456 miles to the northwest of Edmonton or 656 miles from Calgary, but the signs show how Albertans, generally, are quite quick to get on a bandwagon and are quite neighbourly about everything.

To Calgarians and Edmontonians, however, and to those living in-between, what the Alberta government dignifies as No. 2 highway between the two cities is still known, and, heaven forbid it should ever be otherwise, as the Calgary-Edmonton Trail.

Like the Macleod Trail to the south of Calgary, whether it is the Calgary Trail or the Edmonton Trail depends upon which way you are travelling. If you are going north it is the Edmonton Trail and if south, the Calgary Trail. It was the trailway of the settlers, and adventure and fun are still to be found along it although the word trail today is more nostalgic than actual for the route is a smooth, black-topped highway that near the two cities is shoving out its width to four lanes.

Adjacent to the highway for practically the whole distance is what used to be known as the Calgary Edmonton Railway, long since doing business as the C.P.R. The railway, too, has entered into the spirit of giving things pleasing names, something that is distinctive to Alberta out west where most routes and trains are know by numbers or by nothing in particular.

Clicking over this 200-mile stretch of railway in such close formation that one almost listens to the clack of the other, are in the course of a day, numerous trains. Two of the fast passenger trains are known as the Stampeder and the Eskimo. Again this is confusing, for the Stampeder and the Eskimo are exactly the same thing.

This train, northbound, is the Eskimo. Southbound it is the Stampeder. It is the only train in Canada, if not on the continent, to be named after football clubs,–the Calgary Stampeders and the Edmonton Eskimos.

Another train that dallies along between them is known as the Chinook, named after the warm wind which on the coldest day of winter can cause the temperatures to zoom upward and snow to come out of its deep freeze and run like mad down the streets.

As he follows the old trail, the traveller moves away from the broad ranching country that is to the south of Calgary. He moves more deeply into grain country with its colourful fields, and gradually he enters the parklands with their smaller, mixed farms and stands of poplar and willow.

The homesteaders followed first this trail and after 1891 the railway, and in the parkland areas they cleared the land with hand brush-cutters, axes and plows and a great deal of sweat. Money was scarce as hen's teeth, and so were the hens, and much of the business at the towns along the way was done by barter, and rabbits that scurried from the brush provided many a good meal for many a hungry man.

The whole country looked, and is still, a good bet. Men who had grubbed themselves a land stake found the years from 1902 to 1905 so wet and hay so plentiful that the first community of consequence, Olds, about fifty miles north of Calgary, in those years was known as the Hay City of the West. During the First Great War the area gradually changed to mixed farming and with its neighbouring communities today is among Western Canada's finest mixed farming districts.

So today cattle trucks, grain trucks; cattle trains and grain trains—each allowing space for the trucks and trains that move the oil drilling equipment to the pot of gold at the end of the trail near Edmonton—crowd the highway and the railway. It is a symphony of commerce and every town is one of the players, but at Olds the railway engineers are inclined to lean lightly on the whistle cord.

Olds is a pleasant, picturesque place of about 1,800 people who live amid spruce trees. It is there the visitor may enjoy a stop at the School of Agriculture, one of the Alberta government schools that at modest expense train boys and girls to be better farmers and farm women amid actual farming conditions. It is at Olds you could meet a fellow who developed coloured corn on the cob, and it is at Olds that the old-timers, at the blast of a train whistle, will recall the time of the riot over the railway crossing.

June may be the month for brides, but it was something of a shotgun wedding between the people of Olds and the C.P.R. on June 3, 1907. The attendants included sixty railwaymen, fourteen members of the (then) North West Mounted Police and about two hundred people of the town, and, like many weddings, the ceremonies began with reading of the Riot Act.

The people of Olds had grown fond of this particular railway crossing. They said it was a legal crossing. They had graded the approaches, laid plank walks over it and people had built homes near it, believing it to be a permanent thoroughfare.

On two occasions the railway had sought to close it—it wanted to put a switch and spur on the site—but the town people had blocked the attempts. So, on June 3, 1907, Superintendent Niblock showed up in a special train from Calgary along with sixty gentlemen described in the Calgary press of the day as "navvies"; Inspector Duffus, a sergeant, and twelve men of the N.W.M.P.

It was high noon when the train reached town and that was not all that was high, either. Tempers of the people were boiling and they did not simmer down at all when the railway superintendent informed the townsfolk that the railway intended to close the crossing.

A spokesman for the town delegation said the first man to interfere with the crossing would be arrested. Mr. Niblock said they had better begin with him. Members of the delegation said they had no particular preference. After a few such pleasantries, everybody adjourned for lunch but before they did so Inspector Duffus, probably to be on the safe side, read the Riot Act, calling upon all to disperse in the name of the King and if they did not do so the police were to fire.

Promptly at 1 p.m. Mr. Niblock and his so-called "navvies" returned and proceeded to tear up the crossing walks. It is easy to judge in retrospect, but it would appear that the railroaders made the first error of battle. The Mounties took an hour and a half, instead of an hour, for lunch and the town people took advantage of their absence to arrest Mr. Niblock, whom old-timers of Olds today recall as a most likeable gentleman wearing a goatee and a tall hat.

Mr. Niblock, hat and all, was taken into custody but when the Mounties returned from lunch they retrieved him for their side. The town police retaliated by gathering in a special railway officer named Foe and a roadmaster named Bell.

While this side issue was going on, the old-timers love to tell you, the railroaders were busy throwing the plank sidewalk on to town property, and the town people were right busy throwing it back again. But the town people had to give up when they lost their anchor. The Mounties arrested the three town policemen. And to show how seriously the matter was considered, when they applied for bail it was set at $2,000 each. What eventually happened to them—along with summonses issued not only for Superintendent Niblock but also Inspector Duffus—seems to be lost in the haze of memory.

But two things are certain in Olds today. One is that the C.P.R. succeeded in closing the crossing and has succeeded in keeping it closed without further ado. The other, as the Calgary newspaper reported at the time, is that June 3, 1907, will "certainly go down in the history of Olds." And so will Herbert A. Samis.

Mr. Samis could go down in Olds town history as the leading gardener, the man who developed the coloured corn on the cob, or the man who collected all the old newspapers.

People who collect newspapers, like people who collect string, are usually in no position to offer a quick answer as to why they do such things. But Mr. Samis, as we sat in his office chatting about bygone days, offered two pretty fair reasons for having what he estimated to be four tons of Calgary and Edmonton newspapers filed in his place.

He said that his brother, A. J. Samis, used to operate the town's first newspaper, the Olds *Oracle,* and turned it out on a press operated by a treadwheel. When A. J. became Calgary's city commissioner he was so busy he often got behind with his newspaper reading. So Herbert A. Samis kept the papers for him as something of a reference file.

When that need passed, Mr. Samis kept on with the job because it occurred to him that there was the possibility that some day any, or all, of the newspaper plants could burn and the papers would have to replace the files.

For that matter, in Mr. Samis' office you could replace just about anything of Alberta historical interest—if not actually, certainly photographically—for there was a greater variety of things hanging from the walls than you would find in a woman's purse.

"Why," said Mr. Samis, shifting himself more comfortable-like on a battered leather chair, "look at that wolf pelt on the door. Look at its tail. It's been hanging there for thirty years."

"Do you mean the pelt has been hanging on the door or the tail has been hanging on the pelt for thirty years?"

"Well," countered Mr. Samis, non-committally, "it's been hanging around that time, but the tail used to be six inches longer. Cats wander in occasionally and sharpen their claws on it. It's kinda worn down."

Mr. Samis had been hereabouts since 1892, coming into the country from Nebraska with his father, Rev. James Samis, whom he described as a homesteader and a man who started churches wherever he happened to be.

He said the famous Klondike trail of '98 really started down south, as Albertans today claim the Alaska Highway does. He said it went right through his father's backyard. Edmonton was one of the jumping off places, he figured, but some hardy souls toughened their hardy dogs by running up from Calgary in what Mr. Samis described as "practice."

But what of the coloured corn? All that pretty stuff with black and white and red and bronze and purple and pink kernels? That, explained Mr. Samis, was the result of an experiment he started in 1925. He cross-bred various types of corn, some even from the Argentine, to find a corn that would be early yielding to beat the frost and still good to eat. The result is corn on the cob that looks like a revolving rainbow.

"Some day," said Mr. Samis, "somebody will make a fortune out of it. I've given it away to farmers all the way from Calgary to Edmonton. I just wanted the people to have the corn while they were hungry."

Mr. Samis could see some value in everything he had collected. His boxes and boxes of pictures, admittedly, were worthy of a museum. Like the one of Dave McDougall's first ranch building at Sundre, west of town, which Samis described as a log affair with the cattle living in one end and McDougall in the other.

There was something nostalgic about the kewpie doll with the lampshade for a hat, but only a hunter could get excited about "the greatest collection of shotgun shells in Alberta."

"People," said Mr. Samis, pointing at this and that but careful what he shook, "come in here and ask, 'what good is all this?' Well, if you pass through this world and leave nothing behind, what is the good of passing through? I'm just one of those people who've never done anything great except mind their own business."

It was that kind of people who built the country. Just plain, ordinary good folk who went about their work minding their business in the days when to be silent and keep your own counsel was considered a virtue and not the sign of an introvert.

There were people like George Bathe, who ran Olds' first hotel in 1891 and named it, logically enough, The Bathe House. Or people like the early ratepayers of Olds who, on April 12, 1901, passed a resolution by which the overseer was asked to "use his own judgment in regard to levy of taxes up to ten mills."

They made their own way, asked no one for help, made their own decisions and were proud of them for in the voting on that resolution they wrote their names in the column they wished. One was headed "for," the other, "against."

They were the people who came with their hand brush-cutters, their axes and plows and patiently grubbed themselves a home and removed the rocks from it so they could till the soil.

And they are still removing the rocks, but often for different reasons. The people of Alberta today will on occasion go into the fields to get rocks to pile in tribute to those who went into the fields in the first place, sometimes the fields of battle against nature, sometimes the fields of battle against man on soil of other lands.

You can find the result at Bowden, eleven miles north of Olds, or near Innisfail, which is the next-door neighbour to

Bowden on the north, or at a delightful little community called Markerville.

Once each year the people of Innisfail and Olds will gather at the big rock with the people of Bowden. The big rock stands at the intersection of No. 2 highway and the road leading into Bowden village. The unusual appearance of the rock often causes motorists to stop and back up to see what they've missed. The bus company contends it is the most attractive rural stopping point on the Calgary-Edmonton Trail.

It was in 1948 that Vic Shenfield, then vice-president of the Bowden Canadian Legion Branch No. 83, sparked an idea to have a big rock placed at the corner. The village council donated a piece of land adjoining the highway, the provincial government gave a little more and also some highway material for a base. So the big rock rose from what used to be an unsightly seven-foot hole in the ground.

All of this, of course, was after they had found the big rock. Scouting parties scoured the district before they found what they wanted on the farm of Alex Waddell, who was glad to donate the rock provided somebody could find the means of moving it.

It was snugged behind a tow truck for the five mile trip to the village and to get it up Eagle Hill two trucks were used because weight of the rock raised the front wheels of a single truck. This made everyone curious about weight of the rock, which stands six feet high. So they took it down to one of the elevators and weighed it and found it tipped the scales at something like five tons.

When they had the rock in place they called a stone mason from Red Deer, just up the road, to finish the job, but he gave up. He said there was so much flint in the rock that no drill could pierce it. So they used cement to attach the plaque that gave the big rock new life.

As has been the custom for years, the people of Bowden each November 11, Remembrance Day, join with the people of Olds and Innisfail for memorial services. But they are all neighbours and their young men were neighbours, too, so on the preceding Sunday, as a rule, the people of Olds and Innisfail visit with the people of Bowden and together they bow their heads before the big rock that stands in tribute to the young men who served, young men whose memories are perpetuated by a memorial no man could build.

As you are leaving Bowden, going north, you'll notice a cluster of new buildings on the west side of the road. That is the Bowden Institute. It is a place where Alberta is setting the pace for Canada with a penal institute where it will be quite in order for the folks from home to take the boys a picnic lunch on visiting days.

All the accepted rules of incarceration go by the boards at the Bowden Institute, a big plant aimed at cultivating the finer instincts of boys who for one reason or other get themselves into jail.

It is a penal institution with the accent on progress and not penalty. In a large double hangar—the site was a wartime airport—there is a vocational training shop. Of the 508 acres around the institute, 400 are devoted to farming instruction. The place has its own dairy. The other buildings are dormitories, staff quarters, laundry, gymnasium, and stand-by power plant.

The residents of Bowden Institute, all under twenty-five years of age, come from Lethbridge and Fort Saskatchewan jails. They are screened by psychologists who look for the type apt to learn such trades useful to them on discharge, as bricklaying, tile setting, auto mechanics and proper farming methods.

The boys are not pushed into any particular studies, but are assessed on aptitude and given an option. Schooling up to grade eight is compulsory, and voluntary as high as university entrance requirements. The institute is operated under jurisdiction of the attorney-general's department, with the department of education assisting.

The residents have unlimited correspondence privileges. This is designed to fulfil a desire to retain family ties, not break them as do present jail regulations. On visiting days, visitors may enjoy picnics with the boys who have the freedom of the grounds. The boys have radios, newspapers, magazines, a canteen and unlimited sports. They do not wear prison garb, but battle dress jackets with slacks, ski cap, boots and colourful shirts. The supervisors—or guards—are dressed as casually.

The boys you see sitting by the roadside, watching the cars roll by, are from the institute. It is, obviously, a place one could easily break away from. That is one of the ideas behind it. The boys are on the honour system to learn to govern themselves.

And so on to Innisfail. It used to be Poplar Grove. But in a word of the Irish it is Innisfail because it is a green spot. This pretty town, nearly buried in trees, is peopled by men and women from England, Scotland, Denmark, Norway and Sweden. The Fogelvik Farm, on the eastern outskirts, developed by the late Andrew Anderson and now operated by his son-in-law, Knute Magnusson, is known over the continent for its grasses. Wherever men gather to talk Herefords, they bring up the name of W. J. Edgar. And wherever they talk Shorthorns, they speak of Tom Hamilton. They are pretty popular names around Innisfail, too.

It is such a quiet, pleasant place one would wonder where the Huckell family would get enough news to fill their weekly paper, *The Province*. But hanging on *The Province* office wall there is a Pulitzer citation. Alongside it is the office motto, "When in doubt mind your own business." The Pulitzer citation, one of the top-ranking journalistic awards, went to *The Province* in 1937 because the late Ben Huckell thought it was his duty to mind his own business, which is the business of minding the public business of others. When the Social Credit government in that year sought to control the press, Ben Huckell was one of the few weekly editors named to a committee to plan battle. It was such a successful battle that it earned for *The Edmonton Journal,* a powerful daily, a Pulitzer prize. And for the little *Province,* a citation. The Social Creditors long ago got over such ideas.

A few miles west of Innisfail is Markerville, a placid inland community—one not on a railway—that supports a creamery and the usual crossroads businesses like a store and a garage.

At the Markerville fair grounds, which is part of a small but attractive provincial park dedicated to the community's service men of two wars, there is a field stone cairn erected by the Historic Sites and Monuments Board.

It is among the more recent cairns dedicated—on Labour Day of 1950—and it is one of the few in the west dedicated to an individual, Stephan Gudmundsson Stephansson.

All the people who gathered in the grove that day were old friends of Stephansson and they came from miles around to honour a farmer who had loved much more than his beloved soil. In return he had been loved, not only by his friends with whom he shared the necessities of life and the labour to earn those necessities, but by the people of other countries for what today is known as his "magnificent contribution to the poetry of the world."

And that day of dedication when a son, no longer a young man himself, pulled back the flags on the monument, the people recalled how Stephan Gudmundsson Stephansson had gone from his labours in the fields to the flickering light of his kitchen lamp and night after night wrote poetry which in the years earned him an international reputation.

As they gathered for coffee and sandwiches at the cook-house on the grounds where on occasion some of the finest cattle in Alberta is paraded, the people talked of the life and times of Stephansson. They spoke of a man who had less than the elementary schooling. A clergyman had taught him how to read and write, and do his figures. He was a man who saw in the prairies, the foothills, the Rockies and in Alberta's sun-sets what was to make him a poet of international repute.

Stephansson was fifteen years of age when he wrote his first poem. That was in 1868 in his native Iceland. He came to North America with his family in 1873, farmed with them in Wisconsin and North Dakota, where his father died, before settling in Markerville district in 1889. In his first few years in Canada he went out to work on farms in the Calgary district, spent summers with survey gangs on the Calgary

Edmonton Railway, but always in his spare time found the food for the thoughts of his poems.

He cleared his small holdings of brush; he cut his grain by hand at first, and threshed it with a flail. After hard days in the fields he would return to his log cabin, by the light of his lamp would dream of his native iceland, of the stirring things to come to a new country he had learned to love, and in his own language he would transform his thoughts into stirring poetry.

In the years until his death in 1927 he published more verses than such eminent Canadian poets as Bliss Carman, Charles G. D. Roberts and Wilson MacDonald combined. That is no claim of his own, but a finding of Watson Kirkconnell, president of Acadia University.

As all his writings were in the Icelandic language, they were read by few Canadians except those of Icelandic descent. And the pity it is, too, for they were the documents of the hardships, terror and accomplishments of the frontier's colonists.

The writings of this Alberta farmer, however, became of terrific significance in Iceland. Ten years before his death, the people of Iceland invited Mr. Stephansson to return home and he was greeted as a national figure.

People of his homeland loved him, loved his volumes of poetry, but he sadly said good-bye to return to the quiet of his farm and the solitude of his thoughts that in the end were somewhat prophetic:

> And when the last of my days is over;
> The last page turned;
> And whatsoever shall be deemed in wages
> That I have earned;
> In such a mood I hope to be composing
> My sweetest lay;
> And then—extend my hand to all the world
> And pass away.

When the people of Markerville gathered in their little park that September afternoon in 1950 it was with tears in their eyes. It was a little gathering of young and old that tied another tight knot in the chain of Canada's unity. In the stone monument the Canadian government recognized a man who had told to the world the beauties and the opportunities of Canada and the virtues of the Canadian farmers of all creeds.

When the farmers who were his friends, who had shared his hardships, went back to their homes it was knowing their old neighbour had earned a place among the greats of the arts and had, just as he said, extended his hand to all the world. And his friends knew it was a gnarled hand.

8

Red Deer and Rocky

RED DEER and Rocky Mountain House are the teachers of much of the three R's that you learn about Central Alberta as you travel the old Calgary-Edmonton Trail. In Red Deer —midway point on the trail—you have today a modern city of some 5,000 that was born of the farm and made healthy on its produce. And in Rocky Mountain House, some fifty miles to the west, you have the romance of yesteryear that is still realistic today.

Let us stop in Red Deer for lunch. Let us get out and stretch our legs in this parkland city that is as neat as a new pin. It is a city where the air is good, where the birch, spruce, poplar and balm of gilead trees are pleasing to the eye.

Whether you come from the south or the north along the trail you literally drop into Red Deer. And it is a nice place to drop into. It is a compact place, but because it is on the floor of the Red Deer valley and snuggled along the walls of its banks, it seems to appear from nowhere. It takes its name from the Red Deer River, taken in turn from the Cree name Waskasoo, a name the Indians give it because of the number of red deer they found along it and a name still carried by a creek which runs through the city.

The first white people to settle on the city site were Rev.

Leonard Gaetz, D.D., a Methodist minister who left the east because his health was none too good, and his wife and their ten children. Their creaking carts came to a tired halt after the long trip from Calgary in 1884.

They had some neighbours a short distance to the west at what is known as the Red Deer Crossing. It is on the original Indian trail between Calgary and Edmonton and was a place where the river was forded. In the rebellion days of '85 a fort, Normandeau, was built there to protect the scattered settlers. Its namesake down river was not born and Red Deer Crossing seemed to be a-growing. Or bound to. In 1884 it had a store and a blacksmith shop and, historical lore says, even a casino.

The casino was operated in a log cabin by three professional gamblers who in the records are described as "American." This is a peculiarity of western history, too. All gamblers are described as "American." Gentlemen of such profession, it seems, were not produced by the other nationalities that helped open the country. This may, in some measure, account for Canada's odd mixture of gambling laws today.

The gentlemen of the old crossing casino, were, possibly, far ahead of their day. Each evening, attired in evening dress and high silk hats and revolvers tucked in the tops of their riding boots, they would open their place of business to the freighters and the traders. At dawn they would crack the reins to their ponies and high-tail it somewhere up river where they had a hideout. Theirs was purely a night trick and it is rather doubtful if it was at all profitable before coming of the Queen's red-coated men of the Mounties left them without an ace in the hole.

Red Deer has not too much of the glamour of the old west. It has the skeleton of the odd character that it can rattle in the closet, but generally speaking it is devoid of the hell-raising personalities of the ranching country to the south. And those same ranchers had a lot to do with this, too. This land of Red Deer was opened at the time the farmer element was moving to the west. These were the people who put up fences, and the ranchers began, in their own quiet way, to put up fight. The ranchers posted men in Calgary to meet these newcomers who were eager and courageous but ill-informed about the country. The men from the south would tell these men from the east that the south was arid and grew nothing but snakes.

So many of these newcomers turned to the north, a land of brush and trees that was a challenge to their courage and strength, and each who came was strong and brave and they stayed and together they built well.

They built their log cabins and they covered the hard-packed earthen floors with cow hides or deer skins and they made homes. They covered their roofs with sod, cut in such a way the strips became known as prairie shingles and when properly laid they were waterproof and lasted for years.

They came as the buffalo were disappearing. The tree and bush country of the Red Deer is not the native home of the buffalo, but it could be that the big, shaggy animals were driven into these new haunts. Anyway, it was as late as 1886 that the last herd was slaughtered on banks of the Red Deer River in vicinity of what is now Drumheller to the southeast.

There were, of course, what has been described as "some jiggers" among these homesteaders. To some from more staid Ontario of the day it was rather difficult to get accustomed to the fact that your neighbours were not only apt to drop in in the morning, but to come in the back door.

There is, in fact, the story of the woman who returned to Ontario shortly after her arrival in the Red Deer area. She did not return because she could not stand the inconveniences if not the hardships of the day. She simply could not get accustomed to the fact that the neighbours considered the hired man–which they were lucky enough to have, a fellow working out to make his own stake–was just as good as her husband.

Then there was the fellow who throughout the years amassed an estate of $40,000. But when he died the funeral director had a tough job finding six people who knew him well enough to be his pallbearers. But at the other end of the scale was the chap who had a small cabin which he shared with twenty-four dogs and for whom everybody was a friend. When he died the service was held outdoors to accommodate the crowd. If he could return to Red Deer he would be surprised, too. Not by the number of people who remember him, but by the fact that the property he was trying hard to convert into a farm, with the help of the twenty-four dogs, is today the site of a drive-in theatre.

When the Calgary-Edmonton Railway came in 1891, the old crossing looked for rapid growth. But it was the influence of Dr. Gaetz that altered the course of the rails, swung them by his homestead and brought a city into being. Today in Red Deer the name Gaetz is perpetuated in an avenue, hospital and is a family byword.

Red Deer has well kept faith with this family of homesteaders. One, J. J. Gaetz, who soon followed his brother, was so fond of a wooded area on his property that he never farmed it and because of that the visitor today can spend a pleasant time there wandering pieces of original Indian trails and enjoying a little bit of nature in its true state before pushing on to contend with the traffic of modern civilization.

This area, broken by two spring-filled lakes, is today a provincial wildlife park and a Dominion bird sanctuary. The visitor whose interests lean to nature can find many things there, from bullfrogs to deer. It was a scenic spot when Gaetz enjoyed it so much that he would not cultivate it, and the park custodians have resisted all attempts to have a scenic road bulldozed through it. Or even, as much as they appreciate the work, to have young people's camps set up on the lakes. Only one concession has been made. That is a small picnic ground with facilities for wiener roasts. The rest belongs to the citizens of nature and to those who like to visit with them.

The area is about a half mile northeast of the city limits and its two lakes are each about fifteen acres in size. The whole park covers about 250 acres. The area was set aside some years ago by Gaetz, but after his death it lost sanctuary status and in time was sold to a training school for defectives and it soon became a spot that local hunters relished. After the tree stands were threatened by fire, the provincial parks board in 1950 officially set the area aside as a provincial wildlife park and its bird sanctuary status was also returned by the Dominion.

Today it is an area of nature left as nature made it. And the visitor soon finds that unless he has the attitude of the naturalist he is missing much and that he is not quite as observant as he thinks he is.

Over one hundred varieties of birds call this area home. So do thousands of different insects. Bull moose lived for some years in back reaches of the sanctuary and deer are among its residents. On the ground you find two of the orchid family, the flyspeck orchid and ladyslippers, which were once common hereabouts but are becoming rare. There are such medicinal herbs as the purple hyssop, which is mentioned in the Bible. There's the strange little beaver mouse, or water shrew, that requires three times its weight in food every twenty-four hours or it is bothered with hunger, and it sings in such a high-pitched voice that most human ears cannot catch the notes.

Red Deer has something else that the people were soon to hear about, and it sounds a new and high note in education. It is a composite school that was designed to point the educational finger at farm youth of Alberta but which today has boys from the far north packing their parkas.

A sprawling institution of forty buildings on eighty acres of land—an army camp during the Second Great War—the school is attended by students from all over Alberta, the Provinces adjoining and from the trading posts of the far north. The Hudson's Bay Company, which has a financial arrangement with northern post managers to educate their children, saw in it the advantage of having the children under its care in one school rather than spread across the Dominion. The school offers academic and vocational studies from grades seven to twelve, and it has reached its primary aim—training farm youth—by the simple expedient of adopting the semester system which enables the farm boy or girl to obtain an education and still be available to help at home with the chores during the busy seasons on the farm, a tremendous asset in a mixed farming community.

It is simplicity in itself. The school is organized in three distinct terms. Instead of carrying subjects for a whole year the students do two subjects in three months. They then write departmental examinations on those subjects, then start two more. Every subject in the course of studies is available in each semester, consequently the student whose school may otherwise be broken by pressure of work at home, can start at any time.

Composite high schools are numerous throughout Alberta—offering technical and vocational training—but the Red Deer school is truly a composite school because it also offers agriculture. To teach this subject, the school has a dairy barn with a herd of registered Holsteins, a plant science greenhouse and full line of machinery to farm sixty acres of land.

The fees range from $150 per year for students from the immediate participating school districts (Red Deer School Division, Rocky Mountain School Division and Red Deer School District, which is within the city) to $125 for outside students. The rates are assessed for participating districts and parents residing in those districts do not pay individually. By comparison, the average high school education cost per pupil in Alberta is $189. The school charges $22 a month for board for students residing in dormitories and $2.25 a month for medical services.

That, briefly, is the story of the school. But more important is the story of the pupils. The school is taking the shyness out of young sodbusters. The average student is away from home for the first time. He or she learns to mingle and live with others and this is as much a part of their full education as what they acquire from the curriculum. In its own way, the school is playing its part to raise the status of the individual associated with agriculture. And an interesting observation of the staff is that the majority of the honour students have come from the country.

If the visitor is lucky enough to reach Red Deer during the time the summer fair is in progress, he will see first hand just what agriculture means to this community, and just what the city has made out of agriculture. The Red Deer fair is not the biggest by any means, but it is certainly one of the best of its kind in Canada. It is agriculture from the opening gate. Unlike most city fairs where the city dwellers flock for the amusements, it is the attractions of the farm that draw everybody to Red Deer's show. It has all the friendliness and rivalry of the old-time county fair. The parade of beef and dairy cattle on the concluding day is something to warm the heart of the man who developed the colour film.

It was in wandering around Red Deer that I met a man who to me seemed to be very rich. His name was Walter F. Harris and he lived in bachelor diggings at the foot of somebody's lot in a shack that was big enough to be a two-car garage. Mr. Harris had suspended a couple of long calendars to make it into two rooms.

He appeared to be a rich man despite the fact that he said, quite frankly, he had done nothing but odd jobs since 1912. In that year he had had a bout with typhoid fever and when he left the hospital the doctor told him to take things easy. So he took the doctor at his word.

Harris had been in these parts for three years before he entered what you might call semi-retirement. Although he was born in South Africa he spent his boyhood in England and came to Alberta as a probationer Methodist minister in 1909. After seventeen months he decided he had had enough probation so he tried pioneering. He lost his bet with the government that he could stay on a homestead. At least he conceded defeat.

In 1912 he went to Red Deer, took up the business of doing odd jobs, such as writing music and garden reviews for the city's weekly newspaper and on mailing days taking the paper to the post office. He carried the bundles on his head until the paper spoiled the act by buying a cart. Harris always argued that it was the best way to carry anything if you had it properly balanced. His favourite news story of each year has been to review the calendars put out by merchants. Best year he has had was 163 calendars. Lately he has noticed a trend away from leg art. It takes a lot of getting around to pick up 163 calendars, but Harris has a bicycle with which he celebrated his sixtieth birthday by riding the one hundred miles to Edmonton.

What made Harris appear to me to be in some respects a rich man—if you eliminate money as riches—was not so much in what he said of himself ("I've enjoyed life and have managed to eat as many meals as I wanted and to keep alive") but in what others said of him. The little things he had done in his community, such as taking good books to cafes to interest the boys hanging around in good reading and on occasion, as one friend recalled, influencing some to attend university.

When I met Harris he was seventy. Will you be content in a shack with a couple of calendars for a doorway between the two rooms when you are that age? Will people of your community recount the little things you've done? If you were in hospital would a girl drop in with a single rose because it would stand out from all the other flowers? Mr. Harris seemed to be rich because he had all the answers.

You may not meet Mr. Harris, of course. But there is no reason why you cannot go out to see the canyon. A canyon in central Alberta? Just go out to the Balmoral district, six miles from the city. There the gorge of the Red Deer River is six hundred feet deep for a distance of five miles, and half a mile wide. Unhappily, no main road leads to it. Just inquire your way of the farmers.

Or you may be intrigued by the islands in the river. Some are eight acres in size. All are owned by the government and if you are sufficiently intrigued there is no reason why you cannot rent one. Nice place for a summer home.

This business of making the most of what you have seems

to be a habit with Red Deer people. They have certainly made the most of the district which is in a soil zone that has never experienced a crop failure. It has experienced the other vicissitudes of nature, such as hail and early snows, but drouth isn't one of them. The district is renowned for its fine quality cattle and hogs. It produces wheat and seed grains. Its farmers have won agricultural championships, provincially and throughout Canada. The area has raw materials and primary agricultural products in bountiful quantity for industrial development and it is looking into that phase of its economy to keep itself in tune with the rest of Alberta.

A lot of this, of course, is due to the weather. In Red Deer area it rains on an average of eighty days in summer and snows on an average of sixty in winter, to give it average precipitation of twenty inches annually. It does not rain or snow for those days consecutively, of course. Between days of rain or days of snow, there is bright sunshine, winter and summer.

A lot of what the area has in mixed farming is due to the ingenuity of the early settlers. Like the woman who had one hen and somehow managed to acquire a Buff Cochin egg from a neighbour in exchange for some oats. When you had to scratch for everything you got, hen money was pretty important. So you can realize the value of this one egg. No atomic scientist of today watched for progress as closely as that woman watched her one hen setting on that one egg.

The husband of the house, however, had poisoned some oats to feed gophers. He left the pan on a beam, thinking it would be out of reach. But biddy, who was hungry, flew up and had her fill. What the owner soon found was a very sick hen, totally uninterested in the job at hand. There was nothing else for it. The hen underwent an emergency operation. The oats were removed, the crop sewed up and in convalescence biddy was left to sit on that egg and finish the job.

Maybe traditions die hard around Red Deer. Anyway, one of the city's residents is an author of some Canadian reputation for his stories of nature. And Kerry Wood does his work in a converted hen house behind his home. It is a comfortable place, well lighted and decorated and Wood, rightfully, calls it his office. Every working day at 12.30 noon, when the children are home from school, Mrs. Wood extends an arm from the kitchen door, rings a little bell and summons hubby in from the chicken coop where, Wood will admit, he can lay just as many eggs as most authors.

Wood finds the material for his stories among his friends of nature and his friends among the people of Red Deer and westward to Rocky Mountain House, and there, although it is off the main line, is a place to see.

When I was a youngster going home from school with a grade six geography under my arm, Rocky Mountain House seemed a romantic place so far, far away. One pictured it as a place with a stockade and inhabited by assorted characters dressed like Daniel Boone and carrying Colts on their hips and Sharpes under their arms. It is not exactly like that, although it has the aroma. No matter how often you visit there, the romance still persists. But it is no longer romantic because it is remote, but because when you are there everything else seems so remote. Which today is the true test of the romance of its name.

It seems so clear, so fresh and so bright, even when it is raining. It is not in the mountains, despite its name, but it takes its name from the mountains that are so big in its backyard, although sixty miles away, that they seem like one of those old-fashioned backdrops on a theatre stage.

When you come to Rocky Mountain House over the highway from Red Deer you pass the cemetery of this community or that, and you know this is a young country because there are more people in the villages than in the cemeteries.

When you are in Rocky Mountain House and look back to the east, you see the clearings of the farms, lined with birch, spruce and pine. Here and there you see areas covered with fallen trees and brush, and stumps. This is new clearing, for the district is still growing.

When you look from Rocky Mountain House to the west and see those mountains, so majestic, so impenetrable before you, seemingly so strong and so safe and so peacefully picturesque, you feel you can't go farther. You could, of course, but you do not want to. And you hate to turn back. Which is the true test of nature's greatness.

Here is a place where it is easy to maintain romance. The abbreviation, Rocky, carries it. And the weekly paper, *The Mountaineer,* is a natural. But it helps, too, to be able to report such community happenings as that from Ricinus that brown bears were seen in somebody's pigyard; that four cougars were reported and coyotes are bold enough to stay on the road when cars pass. In 1950 there was great excitement when a man shot a Kodiak bear that somehow felt at home far from its home range of Alaska.

In time more people will get to know Rocky. In process of slow construction, what with shortages of this and that, is the David Thompson Highway. It will run from Red Deer, past the summer resort of Sylvan Lake, thirteen miles west of Red Deer, then on to Rocky and, it is hoped, ultimately will continue westward to reach deep into the mountains and grab hold of the Jasper-Banff highway.

When it does it will twist the necks of those who come from the mad outside world and they will race down through Rocky's country. But let them take care. Let those who know it today put up signs along the highway. And let the signs say, "This is nature's home. Quiet zone. Please do not blow horns."

This place keeps the fire pots of history alive today with a couple of old chimneys. They are about a mile and a half south of the town in a small, neat park. The chimneys are all that remain of the Rocky Mountain House fort constructed in 1864. They have been restored to partial measure of their original height from rubble found on the ground and have been reinforced against the weather. Nearby is a cairn, erected in 1931 by the Historic Sites and Monuments Board, which pays tribute to David Thompson, one of the most famous explorers and traders in the employ of both the North-West Company and the Hudson's Bay Company. Thompson, in his travels, accompanied most of the time by a fifteen-year-old Indian bride, prepared the first accurate and scientific data of Canada's western geography. It was from Rocky Mountain House that he set out in 1807 to discover headwaters of the Columbia River.

Rocky Mountain House was established in 1799 by the North-West Company and was for seventy years the most westerly and southerly fort in the Blackfoot country. It was from here in 1802 that Thompson set out on his first attempt to cross the Rocky Mountains. Before discovery of the Athabaska Pass in 1810, the route to the trans-mountain country lay up the North Saskatchewan, and Rocky Mountain House was not only a trading centre for the Blackfoot and other Indians but a depot on the mountain route.

Built nearby in 1799 was Acton House, constructed by James Bird of the Hudson's Bay Company on the left bank of the river. Superiority of the North-West Company in trading led to the abandonment of this fort in 1807. It was re-established in 1819 but two years later, after union of the two companies, the Hudson's Bay Company abandoned Acton House in favour of the stronger fort.

The traders were always having troubles with unruly customers and Rocky Mountain House fort was burned by the Indians but the residents, warned by an Indian youngster they had nursed through the measles, fled. Before they did so they buried three cannon. As late as 1937 the Hudson's Bay Company still had this missing property on its mind if not among its assets. Parties were sent to uncover the cannon but they were not found and it was believed they had been dropped in the river. Residents of Rocky Mountain House for years after took great delight in their spare time in digging around for the cannon and also for a keg of rum that history had it had been buried, too. The rum is still an incentive to find the cannon.

To some extent Rocky Mountain House is a last stronghold

in the west. Until comparatively recently it was the home of the last of Canada's nomads. Some two hundred Chippewa Indians roamed Rocky's foothills, and some still do, and theirs was truly a strange story, the story of some peoples who lived a life of dire poverty and virtual illiteracy because of their faithfulness to the dying wish of an early chief that they fight for the heritage of their people.

Theirs was a story of many sides and one was the question of why they continued this nomadic, fruitless existence when for the sake of their children they could take up a 33,000 acre reservation which had been blocked out for them. People around Rocky who were acquainted with the Chippewas offered two reasons. One was that the Chippewas claimed the country was their heritage and the white man had stolen it without adequate compensation. The other was that the Chippewas believed the area blocked out for them was too far from settled points and would not be productive.

The blocked area is on the Nordegg river, from the north end of the present Cree reserve to the river, and is reportedly the site of millions of feet of marketable timber. But the Chippewas contended it was not suitable for agriculture. So for years they spurned settlement, living a life of wandering the foothills, a life that could at best be described as paganistic under present conditions, a life of ill-health and virtual illiteracy for their children in comparison with the reserve-bound Crees. In summer the Chippewas lived in tents, near rivers where water and wood were available. In winter many also lived in tents, with moose-hides for their beds, but some sought shelter of clapboard shacks or abandoned buildings on farms. In the spring, many, old men and women and young children, would be gone. The great hacking, contagious cough had taken its toll. It was once estimated that fifty per cent of the band's children died before they were sixteen years. Some of the parents sent their ill children to the Indian hospital at Edmonton but they were too far gone for anything to be done to lead them to recovery, and when they died it was a bad influence on the ignorant parents. So no more went to the white wards. They died in their tents.

The man behind all this was old Chief Jim O'Chieve, who died about 1937 at the age of about 107 years. For years Old Jim led the band around the Nordegg, Brazeau and North Saskatchewan Rivers. Each spring they would go to Rocky Mountain House to dispose of their catch. In the thirties white settlers flocked around Rocky and a band of Crees, under Chief Sunchild, was moved there from North Battleford, Saskatchewan, by the Indian department. The Chippewa was moved out because of their coming. They went farther north to Whitecourt and Mayerthorpe on the Athabaska River, but within a few years began drifting back.

White people were inclined to criticize the Chippewas for their so-called paganistic life, but every night before he retired a Chippewa would stand outside his tent, raise his arm to the sky and thank the Almighty for whatever he had received that day. It may have been only a couple of rabbits for the stew pot. If white man stumbled upon one of their encampments at mealtime he would be invited to join them. Before the meal blessings would be offered and, after it, thanks. But the meal would consist of what bit of game the Indians had stored, or what they had purchased from what they made through small tasks performed for others along the road.

In 1930, Ottawa, which could not get them to settle down, found their plight so acute it offered them relief. Chief Yellow Face, head man of the day, refused. He voiced his appreciation for the offer but said that so long as his people could keep body and soul together they would not ask for anything, nor take anything from the white man. They held out for years after that, too.

In Rocky today the wail of saws sings a requiem for one hundred and fifty years of history. The wind soughs through the trees that border the two chimneys at the old fort—on farm property donated to Canada by Mrs. Mable A. Brierley. From the sawmills comes much of Rocky's bread and butter today. From the west, around Nordegg, coal mining helps. The brush has been cleared and many people are farming to feed grain to the town's one elevator, and more brush is being cut and more are coming in to farm.

The country is absolutely full of scenery. It is all trees and streams and amid the trees and in the streams there is game and fish, and the people who come to shoot the game and catch the fish are building a worthwhile industry for the town. In the fall it is big game country. Hunters eager for their quota of one brown, one cinnamon or one black bear, plus a grizzly, flock in by the hundreds. Lately they have come for two reasons. Some want the heads for the trophies of the hunt. Some are looking for extra meat rations to help the family larder in days of high prices. Some even truck in their own horses or ponies with which to haul their kill out from the bush.

In Rocky today the visitor finds the Indian shuffling along the streets in moccasins, peering into the store windows. The squaws carry their papooses strapped to their backs. It is like stepping into the past but yesterday and today are so perfectly and so peacefully molded that nothing seems unusual.

But the place has simmered down somewhat. It is seldom these days that you find a miner, in from the Nordegg areas, sitting on a curb with twenty-three alarm clocks strapped to his body, each set to go off at a different time. Just having fun.

To some of the old timers, the steady settlement has brought ideas of big business. Like the trapper who had his cabin at a fine fishing spot. He thought he would give up the isolated life and move to town so offered his cabin to a banker for $50. The banker did not want to take advantage of the old chap, with whom he had often stayed on fishing trips. He knew some associates in Calgary would grab at the chance to get the place for a fishing camp, so he said they would pay the trapper $500. The old trapper, confused, said he would think it over. Later he returned to say that if the place was worth $500 just to go fishing, he guessed he would hang on to it. There would always be fishing and the price might go up.

The old fellow's outlook on the future just about typifies the place, too. Across from the Mountview Hotel there is a fire warden's tower, and a wonderful sight from it, too. And in the lobby of the Mountview Hotel there is a sign that symbolizes Rocky Mountain House today. It says: "This is God's country. Don't set fire to it and make it look like hell."

9

Home of History and Domain of the Driller

As you move northward from Red Deer you are entering a land that is the haven of the history of Canada's northwest. It is a place pockmarked by names that perpetuate the memory of men who years ago used their influence to weave a blanket of peace for the prairies. It is the home of names that made news in other days and of names that are making news today, for now you are entering the domain of the drilling crews who have brought a new era to the Province and to Canada.

From Red Deer you come first to Lacombe, named after a Roman Catholic priest who first came to the country in 1850 via York boat on the North Saskatchewan River. He was a man who stayed to bring education to the Indians and progress for the whites; a man whose name today rightfully belongs to all of Alberta, not just one community. But the story of Father Lacombe is best learned when you reach Edmonton for it was near there, at St. Albert, that he established a colony and mission from where he extended the hand of friendship to the Indians and the hand of faith to the white men and their brave women who came to develop agricultural Alberta.

Lacombe has kept pace with agricultural Alberta, in some measure has led the pace. It has its own niche in the story of the Province's farm development and it is firmly seated in that niche. It was in this placid but busy farming town that the first purebred bull sale was held in Alberta in 1904. Other places today may have bigger sales of that kind, but there is none that has one that is older.

Here each year a horse sale is held. It is a sale that attracts buyers from all over the United States and Canada for it is second in the world only to one in Scotland. It is here that in 1908 the Canadian government established an experimental farm. From its 160 acres of that day it has grown to 1,700 acres, a tree-lined station that farms the soil for knowledge as a service to the sodbusters. Lacombe, too, is the home of the Canadian Union College, which was started to offer theological training but which today offers a complete training in agriculture and also two-year pre-med course.

It is a young man's town. In 1951, about eighty per cent of its businesses were owned and operated by men of forty or under. Most of those who went to the war returned to the home town to strike out on their own in the business world or to take over from their fathers. What a town has that makes its young people do things like that is something one cannot define. It is something probably best described by the young man who said, "I like it here." Of course, the weather could have something to do with it. Lacombe people are fond of telling the story of one of their citizens who was in Ottawa and went to visit the head offices of the meteorological service, simply because keeping weather records was a hobby with him. He remarked to the chap who was showing him around that he would undoubtedly know a lot about Canada's weather, and in view of his knowledge where, if he had the opportunity, would he wish to settle purely from a viewpoint of having the best weather. The meteorologist, without knowing where his visitor was from, replied, "A little place up in Alberta called Lacombe. It has good weather more consistently than any other place in Canada."

You may go through Lacombe in a hurry. There are

bigger places calling. But these young men of Lacombe like to tell the visitor of what they have accomplished with their aquatic club for the kiddies, of how they draw skiers from Edmonton in the winter with the 800-foot long ski tow they had the foresight to erect on a nearby hill. They like to tell you of how five of their number dreamed up the $120,000 memorial centre, of how they built it from a financial foundation of $4,000 raised by raffling an auto.

There may be other towns with such centres—this one combines Canadian Legion clubrooms, a bowling alley, kitchen, banquet hall, badminton courts, assembly hall and a skating rink under one roof—but somehow in the Lacombe centre there is epitomized the friendly spirit of the prairie's small towns; the spirit that makes people refer to them as "the old home town." It is the spirit that gets things done without too much pressure being applied. And that is one of the remarkable things about this big structure in Lacombe.

In this community, when they speak of volunteers, they mean volunteers for in the whole campaign the committee spent only $300 on advertising for this or that event that helped to raise funds. At one stage, when it appeared too much had been bitten off to be carried out as a community project, the town folk voted nearly one hundred per cent to have the $60,000 rink project become a town proposition.

In Lacombe I met a man who had been a tailor for seventy years and who, at eighty-five, didn't need his spectacles to hit the eye of a needle. Duncan Cameron was a spry, affable fellow who wore two vests when working—he stuck the needles and the pins and things in the outer vest—and who disagreed with the belief that styles changed.

Sitting cross-legged on a table in the basement of his home, which was his workshop, Mr. Cameron gave me a big argument that the old saying that there is nothing new under the sun applies to styles more than anything else. He brought out a book of 1916 styles for women in order to prove it. He had a good argument. In those days the women were wearing a loose swagger coat but which today is simply a "shortie coat." The one change he had noticed was in what a few years ago was known as "the new look" and Mr. Cameron was inclined to take off his hat to the ladies of Lacombe for what he called being sensible. It was not long before they were dropping into his basement shop to have their dresses shortened and to him this was good, for he thought the old look was much nicer than the new.

Mr. Cameron was a lad with thirteen years and a sixth standard education when he became a tailor's apprentice in Scotland. It was in 1904 that he came to Alberta to homestead, but he went back to tailoring after he was burned out the same year he took up the land.

Just to the west of Lacombe is Bentley, known as Alberta's Model Village. It is a nice title but nobody seems to know how Bentley acquired it. There is some suggestion that Frank Thorpe gave it the nickname. Everybody knew Thorpe as "Cap" because he ran steamboats hauling lumber on Gull Lake years ago. Anyway, it is a nice name for the place which is in Blindman's Valley. The valley got that name because some Indians became snowblinded there many years ago. Bentley is in the centre of a rich, deep black soil zone and the climate is conducive to garden growing. Some of the people have had nominal success with fruits and they all give a great deal of thought to landscaping of their homes. They try hard to live up to the name which came from they know not where.

But let us get along. Here is Ponoka up the way. Ponoka is a Cree word that means Black Elk. This town does business when everybody else along the line is enjoying the weekly mid-week half-holiday, simply because it is hog day in Ponoka. This makes things a little confusing for the commercial travellers, who must keep track of the fact that Ponoka has its holiday on another day. But if you have any friends around Ponoka and want to see them in town, you are sure to find them there on hog day.

Ponoka is another of those places that was first put on the map by the Hudson's Bay Company. A farm nearby, on what is the "old road" between Calgary and Edmonton, was known as Fort Ostell. The old trading post, or part of it, now serves as a barn on the Cliff Vold farm. Cliff Vold and his brother, Harry, incidentally, run the gamut of stock raising. Together they specialize in rodeo bucking stock and they have supplied shows all over Western Canada and in the United States.

In that respect they are following an old family tradition. Their father and his father before him were ranchers and riders. The two Vold boys were riders in their more supple days, too. And a cousin, Everett, became a champion in the artful but tough procedure of steer decorating.

Cliff Vold will tell you all kinds of stories about bucking horses. A good rodeo horse is born, not raised, and a good bucking horse would rather buck than eat. Nobody knows why. Harry Vold can tell a good bucking horse just by looking at it. Cliff Vold, on the other hand, goes in for horses of all sizes. He raised what he called "coloured horses"—pintos—for twelve years and in that time had six albinos. An albino among pintos occurs once in every 2,000 births. The albinos always die and they always die, for some reason or other, three days after birth. At least that was Vold's experience. Vold has also raised mighty cute Shetlands and with them he added something new to rodeos. He drives them in teams of four, with wagons. Something of Shetland pony chuckwagon racing.

Most of his Shetlands were sold to people who could afford one instead of a bicycle for their children. He has had Shetlands that were eighteen inches high and a mare that was thirty inches high. They used to be popular among country children as a means of getting to school, but the school bus has cut into that market across the west.

This old barn on the Vold place has an interesting background. It was once the only sign of life between Calgary and Edmonton. It has tamarac beams and square iron nails. Henry Stelfox, who farmed on the land before the Volds and who is living at Rocky Mountain House to the west where he earned a reputation as a historian, did some research into the old building. He found an Indian who told him that during the Riel Rebellion the post had been looted and that some of the Indians, presumably the looters, had been poisoned. It seems the Indians took the poison by mistake when eating or drinking everything handy during their moments of merriment.

This business of Ponoka's hog day is a lot more than just local tradition. What goes on on that day has made Ponoka the leading hog shipping point in Canada. It happens each Wednesday, which elsewhere is a half-holiday for stores. Ponoka business people take their midweek holiday on Thursdays. They squawked long and loud about being out of tune with other towns but they couldn't meet the squeal of the hogs which are quite a big noise with the railway and which insisted, because of its schedules, on shipping hogs on Wednesdays.

Hog day brings around 130 farmers to town from a radius of forty miles and on a good hog day twenty carloads will move out of Ponoka. One of the yards will handle up to a million and a half dollars worth of stock in a year. A lot of business goes on down by the tracks in these prairie towns.

Just along the highway north of Ponoka, at a place called Hobbema, there is big business in fence posts. When you are approaching Hobbema it is wise to heed the signs along the highway that warn of horse-drawn traffic. The Indians still mosey to this little village by democrats and wagons and a speeding car can overtake them in a hurry. In the spring the wagons come in loaded with willow poles as the Indians virtually go to the post. The Indians have been harvesting these willows since 1915 and have made quite a business out of shipping them around the country for fence posts. Some years they will ship out a million at prices ranging from two to four cents apiece. Most of them go to the mixed farming areas of the north, but when the oil fields boomed around Edmonton, so did the Hobbema fence post business.

No matter what time of year you pass Hobbema you will find willows stacked alongside the highway, although the harvesting is always in the spring. The Indians spend the winter cutting and sharpening the willows. In the spring they haul them to the village where the storekeepers buy them for resale and shipment. Sometimes the poles are piled outside Hobbema's stores as high as a two-storey building and for about a block in length. The area is getting a little thin, of course, but it is still a lucrative sideline for the Indians who also ship out cattle and up to 500,000 bushels of grain a year. Which is not bad for a village you can drive through so quickly you would hardly notice it.

The village borders on four reserves and ninety per cent of its commerce comes from the money belts of the Indians. About one hundred whites live in Hobbema, including those at the Indian agency and the mission. The storekeepers say there have been many changes in the Indians throughout the years but in one respect they have remained the same: You cannot high-pressure them into buying anything. They will spend hours looking at things, and when they are ready to buy they will buy and not before. Of late years they have taken a shine to quality goods but the old colourful prints remain a best seller. In his buying the Indian is somewhat a victim of habit. One of the Hobbema storekeepers was telling me that once he had quite a run on packaged tea. When he could not get the same tea in packages he bought it by bulk. But he had a tough time selling it. It was the same tea but the Indians knew a good package when they saw one.

It may not apply everywhere, but in Hobbema at least the Indian prefers chocolate bars to the hard candies—those colourful but tough confections so popular in Christmas stockings—that he once relished. And his fancies have changed from plug tobacco to "the makings" to factory-rolled cigarettes. He has also taken to buying potatoes, something his forefathers never cared for, and he has become fond of peanuts and bologna.

If you hang around Hobbema long enough you will find it is quite a busy little place and most neighbourly. Folks are always jogging into town in their wagons and buggies and on saddle ponies that are always kicking up the dust of its one street, which parallels the highway. You cannot see a house, apart from the agency, for miles around and it is a mystery where all the people come from. They all travel by the same, slow mode and there are so many horses tied to hitching posts and fences that the place has the atmosphere of a movie set.

Big event each year for the Indians is the sun dance, their expression of gratitude to the Great Spirit for the green grass, fat ponies and lots of game. The white people who have watched this ritual throughout the years say it has changed, too. Today it is more of a picnic. The Indians are not as weatherwise as they used to be, either. At least not those in the settled areas. There was a time when they watched nature to figure out coming weather. Now they get their forecasts over the radio.

And so on to Wetaskiwin and the Peace Hills. It was a peace treaty which gave name to this city.

Near Wetaskiwin of today there is a cairn to commemorate signing of the peace treaty between the Blackfeet and Crees. Rather funny, judging by the stories handed down, how the two enemies got together, too. Seems that one night a bunch of Blackfeet camped on one side of a hill and some Crees on the other. Neither knew of the presence of the other. During the night a Blackfoot minor chief decided to take a stroll. Seems that one of the Crees had the same idea. They bumped into each other on top of the hill. They went at it hammer and tongs with their bare hands. They battled for hours until, at point of exhaustion, they sat, or fell, down to rest.

Apparently the Cree, who had his pipe with him and had not lost it during the scuffle, lit himself a smoke. Without thinking, he handed the pipe to the Blackfoot. And the latter, also too tired to care much about the significance of the act, took a few puffs. The result was the famous pact between the two tribes, for to smoke the pipe together indicated friendship. Anyway, that is the legend.

So Wetaskiwin grew amid the hills of peace. And as it grew it wrapped around itself some local lore that is refreshing along this trail of towns that in the main were quite serious about the business of getting ahead. Much of this lore was recounted in the city's weekly newspaper, *The Times,* when it got around to peeking into its own closet to see what it could find to offer the folks on the occasion of the city's fiftieth anniversary in 1951.

Wetaskiwin today is a comfortable sort of a place, a little overshadowed by its big neighbour of Edmonton only forty miles to the north, but among its own people it fits like an old shoe. But it tried out several styles before it got one that fitted and helped it stand on its feet—the straight farming economy.

Perhaps it is in the files of a town's paper, particularly a weekly paper, that one best finds the sense and nonsense a community can accumulate in its lifetime. To look over Wetaskiwin in retrospect it was this anniversary edition of *The Times* that caught my eye. Little items like the fact that in 1902 a music box was the big attraction at the Driard Hotel and in 1906 the authorities denied that an outbreak of diphtheria was caused by a visiting circus using slough water to make lemonade. Or the happy thought that occurred to Chief Ermineskin of the Hobbema Reserve in 1910 when he attended a Hudson's Bay Company pageant and in a spirit of goodwill offered the company's governor the gift of a couple of wives. The governor declined.

In 1913 Wetaskiwin's druggist, H. L. Higgs, was giving away a pair of goldfish with every fifty cent purchase. Draught beer was five cents a glass at the Prince of Wales Hotel and three short whiskeys cost twenty-five cents. And life, with all its international pathos and worry, was good in 1916 when the Criterion Hotel dining room was decorated with drapes depicting animals of the ark interlaced in various foliage effects.

Wetaskiwin's importance in the agricultural picture today is emphasized by its grain elevators and its flour mill, but somewhere throughout the years it was Eph Girling who gave it a big boost. Eph Girling was the city's first Mountie, in the days when it was a town, but he quit the force to marry, a procedure which has in the years cost the famed Canadian force many good men.

Eph Girling's contribution to Wetaskiwin's agriculture was in having the courage to tackle the job of setting up the district's first binder when the farmers were talking up the merits of mechanization and arguing about whether the auto had any merit as a suburban vehicle. Girling set up this binder—with what experience is not recorded—for John West. There was one piece left over, which Girling nailed to the shed door. It seems, however, that Christian Shantz, who bought the binder for $125, did not miss it. Nor, apparently, did the binder.

Throughout the years, too, Wetaskiwin had visions of industrial might, something it is still nursing in the back of its mind, for it has raw materials for such things. As a matter of fact, some of its better buildings are made from bricks that were manufactured in its own brick factory as far back as 1904. Three years later somebody did pretty well with a tent and mattress factory and the same year a macaroni factory employed seven girls who turned out six different kinds of macaroni. That was the same year a rotary steam engine factory was promoted. The plans got as far as the basement when the whole thing came to a sad end because it was found such a gadget was not practical.

Wetaskiwin at one time had its eyes on greater things, too. A gentleman appeared in town, announced he was starting a factory to make automobiles. He called in a painter to give him estimates on a job of converting some premises. While the painter was away doing his figuring, the law approached the industrialist, arrested him for embezzlement elsewhere and that was the end of that.

Among Wetaskiwin's citizens throughout the years was a chap named Bob Edwards. Edwards was a newspaperman and his name is as much a part of Alberta as are the Rockies. Edwards held fort at High River at one time and has gone down in history as publisher of the Calgary *Eye Opener*. Edwards put out such good newspapers that from time to time most of his influential readers expressed great desires to sue him. It was in 1897 that Edwards published *The Free Lance* in Wetaskiwin. The paper was published there but printed in Strathcona, which then was a place in its own right but is today a part of Edmonton.

One of Wetaskiwin's citizens to be the object of Edwards' reportial eye was a homesteader named George Turner. Edwards was attracted to Turner as a piece of news when Turner purchased a billy goat. Edwards reported Turner's acquisition of a "new billy goat" with this thought: "There will be an ideal alpine scene from now on out at Little Pipestone with Mr. Turner roaming on the mountain, alpenstock in hand, at the head of his goats, leaping from crag to crag and yodelling all day long."

A rather unusual sight in Wetaskiwin is trees growing from pavement outside the Alberta Dairy Pool plant. The six poplars were there before the plant and the manager, W. A. MacAllister, hated to see them go when construction started. So a boulevard was built around them. The trees have flourished in pavement pots although they had to be topped when their fluff blew into the creamery.

The Peace Hills, or Wetaskiwin, is the rightful place for a cairn to commemorate the Province's two great peacemakers, Rev. John McDougall and Father Lacombe. The story of Father Lacombe, of course, will be learned when we get to Edmonton. The McDougall story belongs there, too, for in that city is the McDougall memorial church and shrine, a monument to Rev. John McDougall's father, Rev. George McDougall.

The Wetaskiwin cairn perpetuates the work of Lacombe and the younger McDougall among the Indians. Both played an important part in making the Indians the friends of the whites and they devoted their entire lives in pursuit of their respective religions.

The younger McDougall was known as "Preacher John" by the Crees and the Blackfeet. His father came to Alberta to establish a mission at Whitefish Lake about 1857 and another at Fort Victoria, where he remained until 1871. Father and son roamed the plains and parklands and foothills together, establishing missions and converting the Indians, and the son carried on the work alone after his father was frozen to death near Morley, west of Calgary, in 1874.

In that year the grief-stricken man accepted a commission

from the Canadian government to explain to the Indians the reasons for coming of the North-West Mounted Police to the west. His was a ticklish job. Undoubtedly he was the first public relations man the country ever had, certainly the first for a police force. He travelled from camp to camp among the Blackfeet, Peigans and the Bloods, met their leaders at Fort Kipp and as far south as old Fort Whoop-Up. In the cryptic language of the historian his mission was described as "successful." Just how successful is best revealed by the fact that white man's domination of the lands that comprised the old Indian empires was completed in Alberta without bloodshed.

Because of men like the McDougalls and Lacombe, the way was paved to change and develop a frontier. Today, moving northward from Wetaskiwin into the neighbouring Leduc area, the traveller finds the frontier is again changing. This is a change wrought by oil and toil, the tears of frustration and the joys of discovery. It is a change brought by men with microscopes and men in helmets.

There was nothing particularly unusual about Feb. 13, 1947. It dawned late, as do days in winter. The farmers around Leduc went about their chores and the people in the town went about their business. They talked of curling and hockey and the things that help to pass the winter evenings. They gave little thought to the men of an ice-crusted drilling outfit a few miles from town. The Imperial Oil Company had had men like that around this Alberta countryside for ten years.

Their drills had punctured 114 holes in the ground, although in the records of the Imperial Oil Company none was revealed as a good producer. But before the setting sun had streaked the cold western sky that Feb. 13, 1947, the snows had become blackened by fresh crude that spelled the name Leduc as a dateline in newspapers all over the continent.

For the Imperial Oil Company, which had spent millions in exploration, some twenty-five years of faith in the possibilities of Central Alberta's plains had been confirmed. Nobody realized it in the hectic excitement of that February day, but the company's Leduc discovery well had tapped the most significant new oil find on the continent since old Spindletop roared in down Texas way some fifty years before.

In 1948 the Leduc field was extended to include Woodbend. Between the two of them they started the greatest crude oil search in the history of North America. On Oct. 3, 1948, the Imperial Oil again blazed the trail and brought in its Redwater No. 1, in another farming community forty miles northeast of Edmonton. That same year its second well, five miles northwest of the Redwater discovery well, confirmed the discovery as a field ranking among the world's most significant finds. On February 17, 1949, Imperial once more hit the jackpot with its fabulous Golden Spike No. 1, some fourteen miles southwest of Edmonton. It set a new record for thickness of pay zone in Canada with initial potential of 12,000 barrels daily.

No matter which way it looked, Edmonton could see itself sitting pretty. In financial centres of the continent men with vision and millions to gamble looked up maps to see just where Leduc and Redwater might happen to be. By 1951, some $300,000,000 in American capital had flooded into Alberta. The proven oil reserves totalled two billion barrels and it looked like only the first draw from a big well. The pipes of new refineries reared their heads like giant saxophones. Pipelines criss-crossed grain fields, one long snake of a thing started from Edmonton and finished at Superior, a thousand miles east, and the crude that came from under the ground rolled back under the ground to fill the refinery-bound Great Lakes tankers. Here and there along the great length of the line, a common carrier, are taps so prairie refineries may drink of their fill. Ten thousand Albertans were making their living from oil fields that had brought new highways, hospitals, schools to a Province which by 1951 had reduced its taxes by seven per cent, hoped to be debt free in twenty years.

Leduc folk went out to the highway, the old Calgary-Edmonton trail, put up a sign, "the town with a future," soon became accustomed to clothing of drillers appearing on the store shelves, the truckloads of pipe trundling through the town, settled down to a long period of prosperity.

It had become a game for big money but a challenge to the little fellow. Many, like Herb Miller, took up the challenge. Miller had become a farmer at Wetaskiwin in rather a roundabout way. His father, Charles, had come up from Oklahoma in 1906 with intention of ranching. But he soon returned south because he did not like the cold. He had, however, acquired a piece of Wetaskiwin property in a "sight unseen" trade and son Herb stayed to engage in what he called "haywire farming." It was not much of a paying proposition and to help pay for the half section, Herb in slack times would go railroading out of Calgary.

He was getting a little fed up with his prospects, seriously thinking of leaving and, in fact, was mulling it over while sitting in his farm kitchen on February 13, 1947, when the radio barked the news about Leduc. Miller knew something about oil fever because his family had felt it in Oklahoma where his father had been an early banker, doing business in a tent when what is now the state was Indian territory. The news that rocked the Province also rocked Miller right out of his rocking chair. He turned to his wife and said, "that's it." He knew how Oklahoma people by the thousands had invested small amounts for well drilling. He had read of how the Chinese and Japanese had acquired large tracts of land in California by forming syndicates. He knew of how Lloyd's of London split up insurance hazards among other firms. So he gassed up the family car, rattled over the rutted roads to Leduc, was surprised to find the place was not crawling with people seeking options. The average little fellow was too confused to know what it was all about. Miller began a three-year job of going from farm to farm, business to business, asking people if they had any money they could afford to lose.

He was squeamish about taking money and first made sure each prospect could afford to take a chance on an investment. He tossed many nights, sleepless with worries of how they would fare should he miss on his first well. Friends told friends, Miller's scheme grew like branches on a tree and the individual branches dangled investments that ranged from $10 to $11,000. When, in 1950, Miller and his associates brought in Calmar West well there were 250 "little people" waiting around to share in the spoils and to rub oil in their hair. By the time another year had elapsed the syndicate had registered eleven proven wells and Miller estimated 500 people were sharing the benefits of royalty cheques.

But the stories of big riches were few and far between for ninety-three per cent of all oil rights in Alberta are held by the Province so the money that is bulging the treasury will in time return to the people in improved services. The Social Credit government of the Province adopted a shrewd oil policy that provided risk capital with bargain rates but at the same time was beneficial to the entire Province. There was no crop of millionaires such as grew in Texas. An exception was a Calgary man who acquired mineral rights on 250,000 acres of Alberta land from a company which could not raise payment to pay a legal fee. The rights, transferred to the Calgarian years before Leduc, became worth $50,000,000 but the Calgarian continued about his business in a two-year-old car and remained happy in his modest home.

Around Leduc, Redwater and, in fact, nearly every place on the Central plains, the visitor finds an air of expectancy and prosperity. But at the same time he may be disappointed in what he sees. In Redwater, centre of a rich black soil zone, he will find a close approach to a boom town. Oil has turned sleepy Redwater into a wide-awake place of 3,600 people and it has that frontier appearance because it has been impossible for the services to keep pace with the development. At Redwater oil storage tanks on outskirts of the town vie with the old grain elevators to give the place the skyline profile of a prolific producer.

But, generally speaking, elsewhere the visitor to Alberta's oil fields finds that the traditional roistering of a boom area has been beaten down by the reserve characteristic of the Canadian people. There is plenty of physical evidence of a new frontier. Portable derricks rumble over the backwoods roads and highways and everywhere they cast new shadows over the stooks and the grazing cattle. Exploration teams continually roam the prairies of the central plains, the bushlands of the north. Rickety barbed wire farm fences everywhere blossom with prettily coloured papers that show where the teams have gone into the fields. Or, as often as not, probed the ditches adjacent to the roadside.

A few miles west of Leduc, the visitor finds a town of 2,400 people that before oil discovery did not exist. Leduc gets the honour because it gave its name to the field, but Devon is the core of things. Devon, started by the Imperial Oil to house its workers, has become a model town with modern homes, paved walks, boulevards, swimming pool, theatre and city-wise hotel and restaurants. It is in Devon that the visitor meets the full impact of what oil has done to the area. Before 1947, Devon townsite was a barley field.

It is an attractive place on the banks of the North Saskatchewan River, that pathway of the west's early adventurers that goes its own quiet way and amid all the hubbub gets no more excited about things than did Thomas Staley. Along the river banks today you can find half a dozen men doing what Staley is doing—panning for gold but more because they like doing it than with any thought of ever getting rich—but the oil fields enabled Staley to give a new twist to the old setup of the sourdough.

Men have sought gold along the North Saskatchewan for more than fifty years. Some years ago a newspaper reporter who made no more money than most of them was able to live in Edmonton's best hotel because of the few extra dollars he picked up now and again down by the river where it flows through the city. He lived amid pleasant surroundings for quite some time, much to the wonderment of his colleagues, until he was asked to move after the hotel people found he was using their bed sheets in his panning operations.

Staley, however, made a good thing out of old blankets. Before Leduc discovery, the odds and ends of trail traffic crossed the river near what is now Devon by means of a ferry. It was a cable and current operated affair. After Leduc the ferry did not have time to turn around even if that had been necessary. So the Alberta government built a bridge and in the process of its construction Staley, an old-time farm hand who liked to spend his days down by the river sifting water in a tin pan, stepped into the picture.

Before this, Staley had been doing fairly well at his own camp each summer. At this camp he had a mud box twenty inches wide and four feet long with blankets on the bottom and a screen on the top. He shovelled sand into it and a one horsepower motor pumped water from the river to wash it. He caught the gold particles on the blanket. It took a lot of shovelling, but the stuff he sent to a Vancouver assay office brought $28 an ounce and he cleared $6 a day on days he worked.

When the government started the bridge building, Staley became a man of ingenuity. He really put old man river back on his personal hit parade. Gravel for the bridge construction was washed at the site. A long flume carried the water back to the river. Staley lined the flume with 20 feet of blanket. All he had to do was to drop around once in a while, wash out the blankets and retrieve the pretty pieces. Every day the gravel washing plant operated Staley's flume idea netted him an ounce of gold, or equivalent of $28, which he split with the gravel people.

10

Crossroads of the World

EDMONTON was not born. It was made. A lot of muddy water has gone down the North Saskatchewan River, before and since man spanned it with the weird and wonderful High Level Bridge, in the years since man first came to Edmonton by canoe until today when the city's airport, only thirty hours from Tokyo, is one of the major sign posts on the world's flyways.

Edmonton is Alberta's provincial capital and university city, not to mention the time office for the Province's oil development. The visitor soon finds there is considerable to be learned in the city itself. The hallmark of its own education ranges from the fine arts to the crafts of peoples from many lands. Edmonton is more cosmopolitan than metropolitan.

As a city of the oilfields, the name Edmonton today probably is as well known as any of the world's capitals. In ten years after 1941, the population climbed from 92,817 to 158,709 by a Canadian government counting of noses. When the noses of those in the environs are tabbed, Greater Edmonton today has a population of 172,112. But for all of that, it is not unusual to overhear a woman on a trolley bus say to a companion, "I saw a woman downtown today. I don't know who she is, but you must have seen her. . . ." When the current expansion started after oil discovery, many of the old-timers flatly refused to go uptown because they no longer saw people they knew.

Edmonton got its first big boost of recent times during the last war when it was virtually an American stronghold. It was a service centre and also the jumping off place for the Alaska Highway construction and Canol, far northern war-time pipeline and refinery project. There is a saying that Edmonton never learned more nor faster than it did during the war years.

Back about 1912, Edmonton, as did most western communities of the day, thought it was going places. It envisioned itself as the gateway to the north—a vision which subsequently came true—not to mention around and about in all other directions. Like a man in an expansive mood after a good meal, it stretched its suspenders every which way. The gates, however, developed a bad squeak and when the bubble broke Edmonton was lucky to hang on to its breeches although all the space it then acquired is today coming in quite handy. In area, Edmonton is as big as Chicago and it is a good thing because oil is expanding the place so rapidly that all the lots that were vacant for so many years have been treasures. Within confines of the city, however, there still is a dairy farm, the owner and the cows of which consider the expansion a right fine thing because it brought them electric power.

Edmonton was described by a Canadian writer as the boom town that will not boom. That is a pretty accurate description. It is busy and it is growing, but it is doing it in as orderly a fashion as it can. It is however, a city without glamour although it is trying to acquire it. For some reason or other it did not bother about it before, but lately the matter of public relations has become of great importance. Glamour, of course, is something neither a city nor an individual acquires overnight and it is a little more difficult for Edmonton because its cosmopolitan population contributes so many different ideas.

Actually, the name Edmonton itself is without glamour. Old Fort Edmonton was built in 1795 and named in tribute to a clerk, who was a native of Edmonton, Middlesex,

England. Even at the beginning, life was quite a struggle for Edmonton. The Hudson's Bay Company established the first Fort Edmonton. The rival trading outfit, the North-West Company, established Fort Augustus. The two forts were practically side-by-side on the river bank. There was bitter rivalry between the two companies for the rich fur trade of the northwest. To have their forts so close together served two purposes. Together the traders could keep an eye on the Indians, who were troublesome at times, and, individually, they could keep an eye on each other. In 1807 somebody slipped up and the Indians slipped in, destroying both forts. They were later re-established just below present site of the legislative buildings, and when the fur trading companies amalgamated in 1821 the fort sites nurtured the seeds of Edmonton as an actual community.

It was fifty years later that Rev. George McDougall erected the first buildings outside the fort's stockade. McDougall was a Methodist missionary, but the Anglicans were not far behind. Rev. Canon William Newton arrived on Sept. 28, 1875, and within a year had established a log cabin church, named The Hermitage, on north bank of the river, seven miles down river from the settlement. The site today is occupied by the Old Hermitage Farm, widely known in stock circles of the west. The Mounted Police arrived in 1875 and constructed their first fort at what is now Fort Saskatchewan Jail, about twenty miles northeast of the city. A cairn marks the spot but what is more interesting is the fact that it was constructed of stones taken from foundation of the original guardroom and the people who did the work were prisoners of the jail.

The sluggish waters of the river brought the quota of adventurers and hardy first citizens of the west to the community until 1891 when the C.P.R. touched the river bank's south shore with the kiss that was to lead to the death of navigation and the Red River carts as modes of transport.

As the Edmonton Chamber of Commerce says, "The solitary little outpost of the great North-West Territories has become a great sprawling metropolis, gateway to the vast north country and crossroads of the world."

They have had a lot of trouble with the slogans, however. What slogan a citizen prefers often depends upon what business he is in. Edmonton is variously known as the Crossroads of the World, the Gateway to the North and/or The Oil Capital of Canada. With regard to the latter there has been quite some fuss with Calgary, its sister city 199 miles to the south, which laid claim to a similar title in the days when Turner Valley was spouting practically all the oil Canada produced. With the advent of Leduc and Redwater, many of the major oil companies kept their business offices in Calgary while the men actually engaged in production worked in or out of Edmonton. Consequently, Calgary figured it was still entitled to the title. The controversy became so heated at one time that Red Deer, halfway between the two cities, got into the battle with the jocular slogan that it was "midway between the two oil capitals of Canada."

It is in and around Edmonton, of course, where you really see the payoff of Alberta's vast present-day development of its resources. The great new oil field that circles Edmonton has built a city of refineries on the eastern outskirts. One of them, operated by the Imperial Oil Company, was brought from Whitehorse, Yukon Territory, and reassembled in Edmonton. This great industrial area that greets the visitor on No. 16 highway within four miles of the city was entirely developed since oil discovery and it has been such a quick development that the farmer still goes about his harvesting and his cattle go about their grazing within the very shadows of the tanks.

Everywhere you look in Edmonton today, something is going up. Or something is coming down to make way for something to go up. The city, however, is clinging to its low skyline, which town planners say is most fashionable. The visitor finds it unusual and something of a treat to stand in the centre of the city, look westward along wide Jasper Avenue and see the sun set. Rather than go up high, Edmonton is stretching out far.

It is problematical just where this will end. Alberta's

wealth of oil and natural gas is bringing new industries. Some of them handle by-products of the resources or, because of them, can cheaply manufacture other things. Important chemicals not previously produced in Canada will be manufactured from by-products of the refineries. Alberta was extending the industrial hand of friendship to its adjoining neighbours, too, and Edmonton was doing the handshaking. Metals from northern Manitoba were to be refined in Edmonton and wood pulp from British Columbia to be processed into yarn and staple fibre. These projects would mean millions ahead for Edmonton, with a chemical company alone spending $54,000,000 on a plant covering three hundred acres that was before devoted to wheat growing.

There is no doubt that Edmonton certainly is Canada's city of the half century, for only fifty-two years ago it was an outfitting point for prospectors rushing to the Klondike. Murals in the Tegler building, one of the main office blocks, show what Edmonton once was. The murals depict the Red River carts and covered wagons, the French and Indians on portage and the dog teams mushing over northern wastes.

There was a rough period in the interim between the fur traders and the gold seekers. In 1879 the first satisfying link with the outside—apart from arrival of the police—came with construction of a telegraph line from Winnipeg. Bustling about the community a year later was Frank Oliver, who was destined to become one of Canada's best known newspapermen and to whom much of the credit is given for keeping Edmonton pinned together in its swaddling clothes days.

Oliver, who became a member of the North-West Territorial Council, a Canadian parliamentarian and minister of the interior in the Laurier government, founded *The Edmonton Bulletin,* second newspaper in the west. The first was at North Battleford, Saskatchewan. Both of them took advantage of the government telegraph line to report the Riel Rebellion. Oliver's first plant was a log cabin, now on display at the Edmonton fair grounds. His first press was powered by a horse and treadmill and the first masthead was whittled by Oliver from birch because he had no type big enough.

The paper bowed out in 1951 and the explanation of its publisher at that time would probably have amused the Hon. Frank Oliver. The publisher said the paper had gained so much circulation in booming Edmonton that it had become too successful and could not meet the costs necessary for its own expansion.

The rebellion news that was tapped over the long telegraph line brought days of great anxiety for the struggling community. The rebels had sent runners to the Blackfeet country to the south in an unsuccessful effort to stir their feelings. Metis population around Edmonton also made the community a vulnerable point. The Frog Lake massacre did not help, either. It was at Frog Lake, near the Saskatchewan boundary, less than two hundred miles east of Edmonton, that Crees entered the village as the residents were at worship. As the worshippers fled the chapel they were cut down. Nine, including the priests, were killed.

Edmonton was quite happy to see the arrival of the Alberta Field Force from Calgary. Major-General Thomas Strange commanded and the force comprised detachments of the North-West Mounted Police, Alberta Mounted Rifles, Steele's Scouts, 65th Carabiners Mont-Royal and the Winnipeg Light Infantry. They left by scow and wagon transport for the front. On the way they stopped to bury victims of the massacre. They engaged in skirmishes around Frenchman's Butte. It was General Strange's force that captured the Indian chief Big Bear, who was later jailed, and eight Indians who were hanged for their part in the massacre. A cairn near the administration building in Edmonton pays tribute to this force.

Edmonton became a city in 1904 and on March 15, 1905, Alberta's first government led by Hon. A. C. Rutherford, met in the Thistle Curling Rink where it laid plans for the imposing legislative building on the banks of the river. It was on that site years before that fierce Indian battles had taken place; it was there that the first Christian church service in Alberta had been held; it was the site of old Fort Edmonton and in later years became the home of the first Social Credit government in the world.

Just across the river to the south, at what is now South Edmonton, the new capital had a rival in Strathcona, and it was the giant High Level bridge, a black and somewhat weird structure that spans the river, that united the two communities under one banner in 1912.

Until then, what is now the Canadian National Railways entered Edmonton without trouble, but the C.P.R. was stopped at Strathcona by the river. Opening of the bridge brought trains of both lines right downtown. And in the bridge, which is the fourth largest of its kind in Canada at the time it was built, Edmonton got a bargain. The bridge is 2,478 feet long, 43 feet wide and weathers the winds over the river at a height of 157 feet above the water. It cost $2,000,000, of which the Province paid $175,000; the Dominion $125,000; the C.P.R. $1,414,000 and Edmonton $286,000. In return the city got a traffic bridge on the lower level and street car routes—one in each direction adjacent to the railway tracks—on the top level. The street cars stopped operating over the bridge in 1951, when conversion to trolley buses was completed. But before that a street car ride over "the High Level" was a "must" for visitors, but many—along with numerous citizens—would decline the privilege. The street cars ran so close to the bridge edge that one could step out the door and drop clear to the river without touching the ties. For psychological and other reasons the trams crossed the bridge on a left hand drive basis, so the doors opened on the inside of the bridge. It was quite a thrilling ride in a high wind.

Four men lost their lives in accidents in the three years it took to build the structure. The passage of the first train on June 2, 1913, was cause for great celebration. Regular train service began on June 12, 1913, and a motorman nervously piloted the first street car across on Aug. 11, 1913. *The Edmonton Journal,* which in those days was selling 15,464 copies daily and was as staid as ever, took a long breath and said of the opening: "With the blowing and shrieking of many whistles and sirens, cheers from the scores of workmen employed on the bridge and the hurrahs of the two hundred or more passengers, the first passenger train to cross the Saskatchewan River between Edmonton South and Edmonton North over the new high level bridge was heralded this morning." Took the customers almost as long to read the "lead" of the story as it did for the train to go over the bridge. The next day the editorial page in a gay mood reported that "C.P.R. stock has declined over 20 points in a week on the eastern exchanges. But it reached the high level in Edmonton yesterday."

Edmonton today is known as the "meeting place of a hundred races." This is to be verified in the faces and the conversations of the people one meets along Jasper Avenue, a melting pot of the west. It is also to be noticed in the architecture of the city's many churches that range from a modernistic church with a crying room for children, to the huge Ukrainian Catholic Church of St. Josaphat to the quaint Mosque of Al Rashid, the only Mohammedan mosque in Canada.

At the Ukrainian Catholic Church of St. Josaphat the temple crosses soar high to the blue Alberta sky. While it was built in 1947, it has the appearance of greater age. The building was financed by congregational subscriptions and the beautiful church stands as a testimony to the trust of its people that in Canada—which they have helped to develop—they may worship in their own way.

The Mosque of Al Rashid has a congregation of about five hundred, silver coloured domes and minarets topped by half moon symbols. The first wedding in the mosque, in 1949, was a matter of considerable interest to Edmontonians. As the newspaper reported it, it was an impressive ceremony, but the bride took no part. Her father, acting on behalf of his daughter, pledged his word to the groom of her choice while the bride waited in an adjoining room. The ceremony was read in Arabic and then translated in English for a western service for which the bride entered the church with her father.

The congregation is led by the imam, or minister, who

is not necessarily ordained but chosen by the congregation as the most pious, sincere and learned man among them. The congregation prays direct to Allah and kneels in the direction in which it faces Mecca, which in Edmonton is to the southeast. The worshippers, on entering the inner room of the mosque must remove their shoes.

This interest in churches is well in keeping with Edmonton's background, of course. The first building to stand outside the protecting walls of old Fort Edmonton was a church and today it is sleeping quietly with its memories right in the centre of the city. Above the door is the simple inscription, "Methodist church, 1871." It has been restored as a memorial and shrine to the man who built it, Rev. George McDougall. Today the hand-hewn log walls are hung with pictures of the great pioneers, missionaries, traders and homesteaders. Many mementos of the past are kept in a glass case and the little building is a treasure house of colourful history.

And so it is at St. Albert, eight miles north of Edmonton, where the primitive little chapel built in 1861 by that other great Peacemaker, Father Albert Lacombe, is now part of a historical museum maintained on the original site, with a brick structure built around and over it. At St. Albert, where the Sturgeon River winds its way through a valley of poplar and pine trees and where Father Lacombe in 1863 built the first bridge of any size west of the Great Lakes, one steps from today into yesterday and back again with the opening and closing of a door.

On the grounds a cast iron statue of Father Lacombe, with a covering of bronze, made in France and brought to Canada in 1929, stands on the site where Bishop Taché of St. Boniface and Father Lacombe stood in 1860 to select a spot for the mission. The statue shows Lacombe with uplifted Cross and it recalls his act during a raid on a Blackfeet camp by the Crees in 1870. Lacombe, revered by both Blackfeet and Cree tribes, was in the camp but the Crees were not aware of it. When the Crees attacked with savage yells, Lacombe donned his soutane and with uplifted Cross faced the raiders. The night was dark and he was not recognized. The struggle continued until morning when one of the Blackfeet defenders cried out that the Crees had wounded the priest. The firing ceased and the Crees replied they wished to fight no more.

This brave humanitarian in the long cloak directed seeding of grain at St. Paul-Des-Gris (near Brosseau) in 1852. He opened the first school in Edmonton in 1859; operated a horse-driven flour mill at St. Albert in 1863, organized a school for Indians at Dunbow in 1885. In 1910 he obtained from Pat Burns, the noted cattleman, about 200 acres at Midnapore, south of Calgary, where today stands an old folks' home and orphanage and where Father Lacombe died in 1916. It was Lacombe who is credited with obtaining from the Blackfeet permission for the C.P.R. to use their lands. The railway gave him a lifetime pass and free use of its telegraph facilities. In a public notice it attributed much of its rapid drive across the Alberta prairie and into the mountains to the groundwork laid by Father Lacombe.

Thirty miles to the east of Edmonton the curious minded may see the prairie west as it lived and breathed. What is known in the guide books as Elk Island National Park is better known as one of the last homes of the buffalo. The largest animals in existence on the North American continent, these representatives of the last great herds have become so docile and accustomed to humans staring at them that in winter of 1951-1952 when the herd was thinned, they would continue to placidly chew on baled hay that was the bait while a man with a rifle dropped their neighbour.

The Elk Island herd at that time numbered 1,700 animals, largest controlled buffalo herd in the world. About 625, mostly bulls five years and over, were killed. The cutting lasted ten days and one man did the job. He threw hay from a horse-drawn sleigh then took a bead on a 1,900 pound animal as it ate. The hides went to police forces for coats and the steaks to butcher shops.

It is hard to visualize that these animals once ranged in the millions, roaming the prairies in herds that extended twenty-five miles in width and fifty miles in depth. They were a prime factor in physical welfare of the plains Indians and the relationship was perfectly balanced because of the simple weapons of the hunter. White man with superior firearms and links with distant markets upset this balance and by the turn of the century not a single buffalo roamed the plains in a wild state. There may have been an isolated herd of wood buffalo in the vicinity of Great Slave Lake and a few scattered animals in the upper Peace River Valley.

In 1905 the Canadian government was given the opportunity to avert threatened extinction of this magnificent animal. Two Montana ranchers had a herd that dated back to 1873, its origin being in the capture by an Indian, Walking Coyote by name, of four young calves near Milk River not far from the International Boundary. The calves became pets at the Flathead Reservation in Montana. The two ranchers who lived on the reservation realized the profitable investment in near-extinct animals. As the animals owned by the Indian multiplied, they purchased ten head. In 1893 they added to the stock by buying some purebred animals in Omaha. It was from this herd, as it was later faced with dispersion because of settlement, that the Canadian government bought 716 head which between 1906 and 1912 were rounded up and safely shipped to Elk Island to become the nucleus of what is regarded as one of the finest herds on the North American continent.

Elk Island National Park also pays tribute to those who came to settle the Edmonton area and to break its vast country into small and productive farm units—Edmonton's meat packing plants, incidentally, produce twenty-five per cent of the entire production of the western Canadian meat packing industry. One of the park's attractions is a replica of a pioneer Ukrainian settler's home, with thatched roof, log beams, mud walls and earthen oven. It is the first unit of a new Elk Island Park museum.

The highway that leads past the park continues eastward, past Vegreville, one of the largest Ukrainian communities on the continent, and on through Vermilion to Lloydminster, at the Saskatchewan border. There are numerous places like Lloydminster along the boundary—places that straddle the dividing line—and life within them can become a trifle confusing when one Province has a regulation or a tax which the other does not.

Lloydminster is a child of the Barr colonists. In 1902 Rev. I. M. Barr left Edmonton to survey the then Canadian Northern Railway line eastward with a view to settling a large group of British immigrants. The following winter he recruited 2,000 persons in England and with Rev. George Lloyd, led them to Canada. Lloyd had been appointed chaplain to the group by the Continental Church Missionary Society of London. The colonists travelled from Saskatoon, two hundred miles east of Lloydminster, by horse and ox drawn wagons. On their arrival at the townsite, Lloyd established a "minster" or mother church and when the place was named he was honoured in linking of his name and "minster." When the Provinces were created in 1905 the fourth meridian became the boundary separating Alberta and Saskatchewan. As it is the curb on the west side of the main street, logically called Meridian Street, this created all sorts of confusion and the town for a long time had two of everything, including fire departments.

Many difficulties were straightened out in 1930 when orders-in-council of the two Provinces put administration of the place under one body. Today Lloydminster is in the centre of a heavy crude oil producing area and it has two refineries. Much of the output is diesel fuel used by the railways.

For a long time in Lloydminster some of the people were not so much concerned about where they lived as what they could get out of it. A few years ago, when the late William Aberhart became premier of Alberta on a promise to pay everybody $25 a month, many on the Saskatchewan side of the town looked with hunger across the line. Some, indeed, even moved. Nothing came of the promise, and when Saskatchewan's socialistic government instituted a hospital scheme, some people moved back. The town agrees on its administration but never on its politics. The Saskatchewan folk have a C.C.F. government, but that party has failed to gain the other side of the street in Lloydminster.

The post office is on the Saskatchewan side and the postal regulations call the place Lloydminster, Sask. But if you buy a C.N.R. ticket it reads to Lloydminster, Alta., because that station is on the Alberta side. If you get off the last coach of a westbound C.N.R. train, however, you are still in Saskatchewan. Once a passenger bound for North Battleford, Saskatchewan, to the east, was found dead in his berth when the train stopped at Lloydminster. The engine was in Saskatchewan but the deceased's coach was in Alberta. Since there was a regulation against moving a corpse from one Province to the other without a permit, the conductor had to hunt up a Mounted Policeman to give him an okay before he could move the train.

There was a time when people crossed the border—or the street—to marry in Alberta and escape the Saskatchewan law requiring examinations. They no longer do this because the laws are practically uniform. The place has a liquor store on each side of the border and during rationing the citizens were not particularly bothered by shortages. And there was a time when it was cheaper for those capable to stagger across the street before being arrested for being drunk. The penalty in Alberta was $20 but only $5 in Saskatchewan. A town bylaw brought equity in such an important matter.

11

Land of the Blue Train

SPRAWLED across the top half of Alberta, between the sagging line that is boundary of the North-West Territories and an imaginary line that would run, generally speaking, one hundred miles or so north of Edmonton, there is another frontier.

It is a place of riches with which man is still not fully familiar—riches that he is tapping in some areas and in others of which he is only vaguely aware.

Occupying the northwest corner of this frontier, straggling into British Columbia and with no fixed boundaries to encompass the term as it applies to Alberta, is what is popularly known as the Peace River country. It takes its name from the mighty river that is a link in the great Mackenzie River system, but addition of the word "country" is in keeping for it is really a little country in itself, its top half mountainous and its bottom half of the plains.

It is a place that has been widely publicized but with which comparatively few are actually acquainted although that situation has been changing more rapidly in recent years because the highway leading to it is the first leg of the Alaska Highway, which actually begins at Dawson Creek, in the Peace River block just across the Alberta-B.C. boundary.

This country-within-a-Province has become known as the last frontier of agriculture and for those interested in wresting a living from the soil there is still plenty of room and plenty of soil. But the settlers who go in there today, regardless of how they may feel about it themselves, are not pioneering. Fur traders penetrated this area as far back as 1778 and at one of its forts, vegetables and fruits, including strawberries, were grown in 1828 and in 1840 it shipped out some butter.

It has known two types of development and is today tasting a third. The first major pioneer settlement was brought by men of the religious orders who constructed numerous churches and missions throughout the north. They were responsible in the main for the first social development. Following them by many years came those who began to develop the land. They moved in by river and wagon trail and those wagon trails today are the area's main highways. And today, from those trails, bulldozers are cutting other paths for oil exploration crews and at the same time paving the way, as rough as it may be at the moment, for further land development.

The first man of consequence to see what is the Peace River country was Sir Alexander Mackenzie. He wintered at Fort Fork, about eight miles southwest of the present town of Peace River, in 1792-1793. In May, 1793, he met a band of Beaver Indians about two days' journey from Fort Fork and on that site was built Fort Dunvegan in 1805, near the present location of Dunvegan.

Fort Fork was on a beautiful point between the Smoky and the Peace Rivers and remains of it today include two chimney bottoms and three cellars, one of which is quite large. When he stopped there, Mackenzie was searching for the western sea. He had already completed his northern search, which led him up a great waterway that he named River Disappointment, for obvious reasons, but which was later changed to Mackenzie in his honour.

Mackenzie left Fort Fork, history relates, on May 9, 1793, to follow the mighty Peace into the mountains and to eventually reach the Pacific Ocean via Bella Coola River. With nine companions he reached Elcho Cove after a trip of two months. Having accomplished their mission they returned to Fort Fork, arriving there in the beautiful month of September with a good summer's work behind them. One hundred and thirty-six years later a cairn was erected to commemorate the event and the site of Fort Fork.

At the point where Mackenzie met the wandering Indians, Fort Dunvegan came into being in 1805. It was built by Archibald Norman McLeod, a senior partner of the North-West Company, who chose the name in honour of his ancestral home on the Isle of Sky. Fort Dunvegan became the centre of fur trading on the Peace. The Hudson's Bay Company took it over in 1821 and it was in operation until abandonment in 1918.

The men of old Fort Dunvegan were far-sighted. While man today still wonders about the potentialities of the whole country, Dunvegan's early residents raised strawberries, raspberries, cherries and some vegetables in 1809. As the years went on, the missionaries and traders of both Fort Fork and Dunvegan grew excellent crops of spring wheat and thus began the land development.

In 1896, an Anglican missionary, Rev. Gough Brick, won a world's championship with a sample of wheat grown at his Shaftsbury Settlement, at Fort Fork, and shown at an international seed exhibit in Chicago. This rang a bell for the whole area, but it was not heard too far in those days. It was not until 1926 that the words Peace River Country really became magic. That was when Herman Trelle, of Wembley, in the Grande Prairie area, took world championships in wheat and oats at Chicago and people wondered just what kind of a place this was.

The area did not actually attract a great many settlers until after the Edmonton area was more fully settled. A few hardy souls ventured north in the years immediately preceding the First Great War. The 1911 census showed that about 2,000 persons, chiefly traders, missionaries and Indians, were living in this new land. By 1921 there were about 20,000 persons and today the population is greater than that of the city of Edmonton.

For those who visit this area, some three hundred miles to the northwest of Edmonton, there are many surprises. You can go a lot farther north by plane or river boat, of course, but even in the Peace River block you have that odd feeling of sitting on top of things. It is reputed to be a land of great beauty and like most places, in some respects it is and in some respects it is not. Its winters are by no means mild but they are not too rough for there is little snow, winds are moderate, blizzards are few and the winter is well broken by chinook winds that come over the mountains from the Pacific.

The greater portion of the country is wooded—white spruce, poplar, aspen—and this is a surprise to most visitors who do not associate a wooded area with grain production. Mixed farming, naturally, is the best bet for on a mixed farm the farmer has more than one string for his bow. Practically every farm has a poultry yard and a kitchen garden and it is obvious that in this country, unlike the southern plains, the farmer lives on his farm.

Up here there is something about the sky that gets you. It is as high and as wide as on the prairies, but its golds and its blues and its pinks come right to earth to make pretty ribbons of the rivers. It is the land of the startling sunrise, the kind that stretches across the horizon like a bright afghan hung from the sky. One of the country's greatest sights is at Peace River town. The sweep of the Peace River valley seems endless, and as you come down the big hill by train or car, the lights of the town are like twinkling toes at the foot when viewed in dawn's early light.

Peace River town traces its birth to Fort Fork and Shaftsbury Settlement and even today there is something of the frontier about it. It is a place that seems in the throes of building forever. On its streets at night there is not so much neon that it is commonplace and yet there is not so little that it is noticeable. It is a busy place. There were in 1951 at least sixty-five oil exploration camps in the area. The bull-dozers were blazing new trails into the bush, making things easier for the settlers who would follow and who would find things not quite so lonely as the first of their kind. When a government telegraph line was strung through the area one early settler had his home made a station and his wife trained as operator. By that means he made a little extra money, but just as important he found himself with a little extra company now and again. But today, across the combined railway and traffic bridge that spans the Peace River at a height of 75 feet for 1,700 feet and cost a million dollars, a control tower clocks 500 vehicles every twenty-four hours, opens and closes gates at each end so trucks and trains do not get mixed up with each other.

The vehicular traffic is going to the farms, the oil camps, nearby communities such as Fairview, where the Alberta government in 1951 opened a school of agriculture that is one of the best in the country, and to Grimshaw, fifteen highway miles from Peace River, a farming community which is feeding the life blood of a new nation over a 384-mile highway northward into the wilderness of the North-West Territories at Hay River on Great Slave Lake.

This is a great Canadian job, a highway that slashes through forests and crosses muskeg to form a supply route for northern industry. It carries mining machinery, provisions and supplies to the port of Hay River for trans-shipment northward to Yellowknife. It moves fish, fur, lumber, minerals and farm produce. It means that mines no longer have to fly heavy machinery into the north. It goes by road then by boat from Hay River. It has made such places as Manning (named after the Province's premier); Keg River and Fort Vermilion into agricultural centres instead of outposts. Where limited supplies of fish used to be taken in summer from Great Slave Lake and moved by the Slave and Athabaska Rivers to Waterways, in 1950 the Mackenzie Highway, as it is known, carried eight million pounds of whitefish and trout worth $612,000 to Grimshaw.

To build this highway was a big job. Construction was started in the fall of 1946 and the road, now all-weathered, was completed in 1948. Survey parties that began work in 1938 were away from civilization for five months at a time. They carried their own provisions. One that found its cache of supplies had rotted, lived on short rations for five weeks. The route partly follows an old winter tractor-train road over miles of muskeg and rolling hills, but where the old trail wandered aimlessly through the wilderness, a new route was plotted.

The route was primarily for a winter road, but the surveyors realized that in time it would be the basis for a highway and wherever possible they followed high levels of land to avoid muskeg. Today the tourist seeking new horizons finds them along the Mackenzie Highway. It leads him to two of the most scenic spots of the north, the Louise and Alexandra Falls. The Louise Falls is 46 feet high and the Alexandra drops 106 feet. Both are on the Hay River within the North-West Territories and until the past decade were unknown.

The highway, costing $4,300,000, was a joint effort of the Canadian and Alberta governments. Building 234 miles south of the territories boundary cost $2,850,000 and the Province paid fifty-two per cent. The Dominion bore the entire cost of the eighty-one miles within the North-West Territories. The Alberta section is maintained the year round by the Province and the territories section by the Dominion.

It was once a dream, but there it is today on the ground, and those who toiled in its building will never forget the two Métis. Many of the men in the survey parties were Métis. Across the north they are known for their strength and endurance. In the final survey party, two Métis were hired to fell trees. They worked as a team and seemed to get along pretty well together. They cut a survey line five feet wide and 150 miles long through the wilderness without asking for help, or, seemingly, to think it was much of a chore.

Years ago men toiled to build railway lines into the Peace River country and should you look at a timetable of the Northern Alberta Railways today you would find that the map that illustrates its routes runs clear to the Arctic Ocean. The railway, of course, does not go nearly that far, although it does tap a wide area out of its home terminal at Edmonton. The map is just a sly suggestion that the railway draws produce from just about everywhere north.

Built by wheat and timber and fish, and nurtured by war and the atom bomb, the Northern Alberta Railways has grown from something nobody wanted to something the country cannot get along without. It was the N.A.R., or its component parts at least, that helped open the great country of the Peace and Athabaska Rivers to the northwest and north of Edmonton. It was the N.A.R. that was the cart horse for building of the Alaska Highway and with the winter road that became the Mackenzie Highway, the Canol pipeline of the last war.

During the last war it was the baby of the top brass of Ottawa and Washington. Things of destruction moved over its rails. Today it moves the products of a peaceful country. But it is still a vital link in the defence of the free worlds. At Waterways, one of its terminals north of Edmonton, it meets the boats that bring the pitchblende deposits of Port Radium down the 1,360 miles of the Mackenzie River system. When loaded to N.A.R. cars the deposits move another 304 miles over muskeg, through forest and farm country to Edmonton where Canada's two major railways grab hold of it to move it to plants where it is reborn in this atomic age.

For building of the Alaska Highway, the N.A.R. hauled equipment 495 miles to Dawson Creek from Edmonton. That leg of the road, which branches off at McLennan to serve Peace River town and Grimshaw in one direction; Grande Prairie—so named because it is the most extensive area of treeless plains in the whole block—and Dawson Creek in the other, when coupled with the Waterways leg out of Edmonton, gives the N.A.R. 922 miles of right-of-way. And it touches virtually everything worthwhile, including oil on fringes of the fabulous Redwater field at Bon Accord and Excelsior, some twenty-five miles north of Edmonton.

The N.A.R. has not had such riches all its life, of course. It comes of poor parents. People were interested in building railways to open new country when what is the N.A.R. first saw the light of day. The prospector and trapper and later the farming pioneer were the only people with any desire to go north. The country was well suited for railway construction and various groups that eyed its possibilities eventually promoted such links as the Alberta and Great Waterways

Railway; the Central Canada; Pembina Valley and the Edmonton, Dunvegan and British Columbia Railway. Oddly enough, while it was the last war that put the N.A.R. on the map, it was the dregs of the First Great War that resulted in the various companies feeling the real pinch and in 1920 they appealed for help to keep operating.

In 1929 the Canadian government incorporated the Northern Alberta Railways, which wrapped up all the rights-of-way into one parcel and which in turn was taken over jointly by the Canadian Pacific and Canadian National Railways for $25,000,000. The N.A.R. has treated the two major systems pretty well in return. Its yearly revenues since 1939 have fluctuated from $2,000,000 to $11,500,000, the biggest year being 1943 with the war movements. The war, as tough as it made things, brought improvements to the road. It was such a vital link it had practically anything it asked for. So today 85- and 100-pound rails carry its swaying freights and its passenger trains of royal blue, a most distinctive colour. The passenger trains are not strictly deluxe, mind you, but they serve the purpose. So many heavy lumberjacks and prospectors have ridden the sleeper seats that they sway in the middle. When the berths are made up and a mattress placed over the curvature, the occupant has a pleasant but bouncy ride. On the N.A.R. upper berths, being solid, are more comfortable.

Up and down the line they never tire of telling the story of Twelve Foot Davis. Davis today lies asleep on a hill overlooking Peace River town. He was an American who loved the Canadian northwest and the spot where he is buried was the place he loved the most. Twelve Foot Davis was no giant. He was a man of moderate stature, born in Vermont in 1820. His proper name was H. F. Davis but nobody in the north knew it after he took on the Twelve Foot handle.

Davis came into the northwest with the Cariboo gold rush of 1849. Gold-hungry men then flocked into British Columbia by the thousands. Trouble with Davis was that he was at the tail-end of the flock. When he arrived, the best land had been staked. But Davis was a man with a keen eye. Looking over a string of claims, he noticed that two of them seemed to be larger than the law allowed. He measured them, found that they were twelve feet larger. So he staked the twelve-foot strip between the two and from it took out $20,000 in gold, went down in the history of the northwest as Twelve Foot Davis.

Davis was also a trader. He would buy necessities in Edmonton and haul them by pack horse to Fort Vermilion and beyond. He died at Lesser Slave Lake in 1893 and was originally buried there but an old friend had made a promise to Davis that he would see he was buried on the highest point overlooking the beautiful Peace River in the vicinity of Peace River town. The promise was kept. Davis' remains were transferred and his gravestone today is in the form of a tree trunk and engraved on it are the words, "Pathfinder, pioneer, miner and trader. He was everyman's friend and never locked his cabin door."

The spirit of such people still lives in the Peace River country and in the Athabaska country to the east, an area along the Athabaska River about 100 miles directly north of Edmonton. This is truly a cosmopolitan area. Settled by Europeans, French, British and even Negroes who fled the Jim Crow laws of the southern United States, it is a lumbering and farming community, a place where one farmer was so wedded to the land that he loved to go around in his bare feet and twitch his toes in the soil. As the soil of this bush country had put him in a position where he could write a cheque for $20,000, with or without his boots on, he obviously had no intention of getting a divorce, either.

The history of Athabaska goes to 1862 when it was a Hudson's Bay Company reserve and the company trailed stuff in from Edmonton to barge it northward on the Athabaska River. Between 1900 and 1914 there were so many traders operating out of Athabaska Landing, as it was known, that five boats plied the river to McMurray and the river banks echoed to the barge builders' banging. The railway came in 1912 and the town prepared for big things. The vision of the pioneers was broader than the prairie sky. J. P. Evans, the town's genial secretary-treasurer for years, well remembers the big boom. Athabaska assessment notices were mailed to people living in Brisbane, Hong Kong, England, or almost wherever the mails would carry some well-worded literature. Land sold at auction for as high as $7,000. Then came the first war and the town was so broke, as Mr. Evans recalled it, "we were practically taking in each other's washing." Mr. Evans still had a job, however. He became the administrator and conducted the town's affairs from 1919 to 1928, and when it took over its own government he stayed on the job to watch it prosper.

The evolution of farming and lumbering helped to bring it back. In the early days logs were floated down river to Athabaska's two mills. Gradually, logging got too far from the river. Now they take the portable mills to the bush, truck out the product and dry pile it at the town's three planing mills. They found a way of handling the farming land, too. The first wheat crop was grown in 1908. Farming was none too successful because the soil was sub-marginal. The farmers turned to clovers, which put nitrogen back into the soil, and from that to other legumes, such as alfalfa, and today ninety per cent of the area's seed is exported to the United States and an acre of once despised land now often nets $130. The people are now worried that it may have become too much of a good thing. There is evidence everywhere of new breaking and thoughtful citizens ponder the possible consequences of the loss of so many trees. But the growing of feed and seed has resulted in another evolution. It has brought diversified farming on a large scale that means the area is on a sound footing.

It is rather unusual this far north to find so many people planted firmly on the farm. Near Athabaska there is a community known as Amber Valley, an apt name for a colony of Negro farmers, and it is a valley whose history is probably best told in the life story of J. D. Edwards. Edwards is one of its leading citizens and as he sat on a rail fence and looked around his farm, he told me he had no reason to be envious of his brother in Oklahoma City who had built a $500,000 hospital because he could not get his sick wife into the one the white folks had built.

Mr. Edwards and his neighbours have no trouble getting their sick into the white folks' hospitals in this country. Theirs, too, is the story of a group of people who fled the Jim Crow atmosphere of Oklahoma when it grew from Indian territory to statehood in 1907.

Edwards was just nineteen years old then, but he remembered that the Negro people were segregated and a group of them formed a colony and moved to Canada because they "had had a taste of freedom and knew what it meant." Edwards was with the colonists who reached Edmonton in 1910. Some went to Wildwood, west of Edmonton; some to Clyde, Alta., and others eastward to Maidstone, Sask. About 300 went to Athabaska. They practically walked out to where they began farming. In those days you could not see 100 yards ahead for timber. Today there are 75 to 100 acres broken in every quarter section—the result of back-breaking work with grub-hoe and axe—and in some areas the clearings are so broad it looks like prairie.

Most of the people farm a quarter section. Edwards is one of the bigger farmers with seven quarters. Their community has a high and elementary school. It had a Negro teacher for eighteen years but two white teachers took over. At one time, only four of the forty-eight pupils were of white parentage. In the years some young people left the community to seek their fortunes elsewhere. One of Mr. Edwards' boys, educated in Alberta, is practicing medicine in the United States. Those who left liked Canada but they disliked the cold or felt there was not too much opportunity in salaried jobs which were limited chiefly to porters positions on the railways.

Mr. Edwards told me that he had not done as well as his brother, W. J. Edwards, but he was not envious. His brother started life as a $9 a week junk collector, then got into the business for himself. After Pearl Harbour he made a fortune and that is how he could afford to build a $500,000 hospital for Negro people of Oklahoma City after he could not get his wife into one of the others.

I will never forget sitting on the rail fence chatting with Mr. Edwards that evening. He made no pretence of having $500,000 although he thought he was more fortunate than many people because he could get a loan from the bank on his reputation. What appealed to me was the obvious pride of the man as he looked around. He leaned on the fence post and said, "All this is mine." It was not so much what he said. It was the way he said it.

Far to the northeast of Athabaska—or along the N.A.R. out of Edmonton and through Lac la Biche, where the highway ends—you can find another pot hanging on Alberta's rainbow. There, at McMurray, are the fabulous tar sands, once described as the "empire's ace in the hole." It is an oil reserve with a potential variously estimated up to 250,000,000,000 barrels of crude. The point is just how to get it out. And so long as oil is developed more quickly and cheaply down south, in all likelihood it will remain as a reserve for the time being.

Nature put the tar sands there, but mankind has known about them for at least 150 years. Early fur traders reported the wonders of the country where oil slicks dotted the rivers. A geological survey was made in 1875 and some hardy souls in 1894 attempted to drill out the oil. This was unsuccessful. Since 1924 the provincial and federal governments have worked with pilot plants on schemes to process the sands. These schemes bore fruit, but the fruit was frosted. What to do with it after you have got it? The most recent report on the sands, in 1951, came from an eminent Canadian petroleum engineer, Sydney M. Blair, of Toronto, who surveyed the economics of the whole field at the invitation of the Alberta government. Blair reported that in his opinion production and transportation were feasible at a profit.

The sands cover an area of 30,000 square miles and are from 10 to 225 feet deep. The district is isolated. Railhead is at McMurray, a connection with Edmonton, but the sands are fifty miles north of that and swampy terrain makes surface transportation difficult. The Blair report contended it was feasible to construct a refinery at the site and a pipeline to move the oil to Edmonton. Blair foresaw a site refinery costing $45,000,000 and a pipeline to Edmonton costing $5,000,000. He estimated that the oil, which has a blend more valuable than that of the Leduc field, could be transported, after extraction, at an estimated cost of $3.10 a barrel and even if taken to the head of the Great Lakes over the existing pipeline from Edmonton it would bring a value of $3.50 a barrel. A valuable by-product, the report indicated, was enough sulphur to supply all Western Canada.

Experiments conducted by the National Research Council at a pilot plant revealed that 420 tons of oil sand per day yielded 250 barrels of crude. This was achieved through what is known as a fluidized sand process. In layman's language it is simply placing the sand in huge pots through which hot air is blown. At 500 degrees the sand appears to boil, the gasoline is distilled and then recovered by condensation. Up to 76 per cent by volume of the oil in the tar sands was recovered in pilot plant tests. The experiments revealed another important factor, too. The sand particles which remain after the processing are coated with a thin film of coke which could be used to stoke the furnaces necessary to provide heat for the actual distillation process. There would be no need to import fuel which would be a major item in view of the fact the refinery would be operated under Arctic conditions. Today financial interests have shown renewed interest in this strange part of Alberta where the earth is black and soaked, where the rivers that flow to join the mighty Athabaska carry oil slicks, and where, when you rub your hands in the sands the oil comes off. Oil men, it seems, still prefer to dig a hole in the ground to force up what is under the ground. At the tar sands they would have to get acquainted with a proposition of mining oil. If the area was developed it would become dotted with open cut pits. But, immediate development or not, it is a cinch the stuff is not going to run away and it will be there should the continent need it.

Those are a few of the things of which man is aware in this great north country of Alberta. And the term north country is a misnomer, too. The traveller may figure he is getting north when he strikes out from Edmonton for the Peace River or Athabaska countries. But when he gets 70 miles north of Edmonton, on his way to Athabaska, he comes to a little cross-roads community known as Meanook and gets a surprise.

Meanook is a Cree name that means beautiful valley and the Crees had a good word for it. On Alex Nimco's garage at Meanook there is a sign that indicates this little community is the "centre of Alberta." The residents say that if anybody wants to dispute their claim they will gladly have the whole Province measured. And if they are right, it only proves that in Alberta man has come a long way but he still has a long way to go.

12

Men and Mountains

. . . . the mountains shall bring peace to the people.

They also bring millions of dollars to Alberta. For the Province that has everything else and all this, too, the Rockies are a vital vertebra that stretches from the international boundary to a point parallel with Edmonton where, because of a slanting boundary line, they become the property of British Columbia. But where the mountains stop, something else begins for Alberta which rightfully makes a great noise about the productivity of its Peace River country that occupies the northwest corner.

The beauties of the Alberta mountains have been described as one of nature's greatest shows on earth and it is a shame to portray them in the drab and dreary figures of statistics. But it is to them that Alberta owes the fact that it leads the Prairie Provinces in international border traffic. Of late years the oil has made the position more secure. In 1950, which is the latest on record, there were 1,711,999 admissions from the U.S. through prairie border points. Of that number, 706,915 entered by Alberta stations. Next in line was Manitoba with 383,616. That, of course, does not take into account the numbers who entered Alberta from the western United States by way of British Columbia points, or those who came by train and auto from other parts of Canada to visit this wonderland high in the skies that, while it is part of Alberta, is rightfully the property of all Canadians.

If Canada at any time in its history ever displayed foresight it was when the mountain territory of the west was set aside as national parks for the pleasures of its people. Some of those parks are in British Columbia. As a matter of fact, British Columbia and Alberta share nine of Canada's twenty-seven national parks. And the three big ones of the west are in Alberta at Banff, Jasper and Waterton.

In this mighty fortress of rock are the beginnings of many things, little and big. Little drips from the mountain snows become tiny streams that become mighty rivers, flowing to the Arctic, Hudson Bay, the Gulf of Mexico and the Pacific Ocean. In the beginning of this country's time, as known by man today, those rivers were the routes of the explorers who followed them to disappear bravely into the mountains and set the pattern for the commerce that now flows through the passes.

What those men found helped those who followed to break down this great barrier with railways and later highways running from east to west. The Banff-Jasper highway slices it in the middle and in the south it is a connection with the Windermere Highway that does the same thing for British Columbia's Kootenay Park.

The most southerly of the Alberta parks is Waterton, which Canada shares with the United States. The American park is known as Glacier National Park. The Canadian park was set aside in 1895 and today covers 204 square miles along the eastern slope of the Rockies. Its mountains rise almost abruptly from the plains and their remarkable colouring of purple, green and gold gives the peaks a warm and brilliant tone. Some have sharp pyramids formed of yellow shale outcroppings which glisten in the sunrise and sunset, while others have summits and slopes banded with red.

Since 1932 the proper name of the area has been Waterton-Glacier International Peace Park but it has been rather difficult to get this mouthful in the public mind. It was in that year that the area was established by Canadian and

American legislation as a peace park. It was set up as such on June 18, 1932, and is the first of its kind by a month or so. The international peace gardens in Manitoba were set up on July 14, 1932. Each year services to commemorate the long peace between the two countries are held at the park, the guest speaker and the service alternating on each side of the boundary.

But to simplify matters for a mind's eye ride through these beautiful parks, it might be just as well to start at the top, at Jasper National Park, the town of which is Jasper, a Canadian National Railway divisional point in a broad valley at an elevation of 3,470 feet about 235 miles west of Edmonton. The history of Jasper, at least as a name, goes back to 1811 when it was a fur trading post. What is today Jasper National Park was set aside in 1907 by the Canadian government. It was originally larger than the state of Connecticut but boundary revisions saw it settle down to its present 4,200 square miles which encompass an area larger than the states of Delaware and Rhode Island combined.

Within the park are cairns to mark the sites of two trading posts built by the North-West Company. One was Jasper House and the other Henry House. The former was named after Jasper Hawes, a fur trader from Missouri who married an Indian woman and raised a large family which was grouped around him when he perished as his raft was slashed to pieces while he made his way along the Fraser River. A cairn erected in the park adjacent to the Jasper Highway near the mouth of Rocky River pays tribute to the post.

A route to the Columbia River through the Athabaska Pass was pioneered in 1811 by David Thompson. In 1826, a second pass, the Yellowhead, was discovered and Jasper House, built in 1813, was until 1884 the main support of the trade route across the mountains and for all persons journeying through the two passes. Henry House, on the other hand, while constructed in 1811, never approached the importance of Jasper House and it was abandoned a few years after it was built.

Throughout the years men whose names have gone down

in Canadian history traversed this country. More than one hundred years ago a Belgian missionary, Father de Smet, spent a month around what is now Jasper. It was a jumping-off point for the explorers David Thompson and Simon Fraser, whose names live in the tumbling rivers they followed. At one time there came David Douglas, a botanist whose name was given to the giant fir tree. In 1862, after gold was found in British Columbia, wealth-hungry men making a hazardous overland trip from the east reached Jasper's confines to make their way through the Yellowhead Pass to the Cariboo country, and their epic journey from Ontario is commemorated in a monument at Jasper's C.N.R. station. Also at the depot, as well photographed as the mountains themselves, is a totem pole brought from Queen Charlotte Islands in 1915. It belonged to a family of the Masset Haida Indians. Totemism, now extinct, was once universal among North Pacific Coast Indians and the figures on the pole do not represent deities, as generally believed, but crests of these particular people.

This particular totem pole is one of the finest in existence and is of great age. Totem poles were, to their makers, really memorial columns, intended to preserve the memory of tribal leaders and to secure public acknowledgement to the title of their successors. The crests used on them are somewhat in the nature of those on the coats of arms of the European aristocracy. In the case of the northwest coastal tribes, however, the noblemen owned many crests and the origin of each was explained in a long myth which was preserved in the memory of owners and often rehearsed at public functions.

After the first flush of travel around Jasper, things got rather quiet. It was not until shortly after the park was established that the railways came. The Grand Trunk Pacific and the Canadian Northern—now the Canadian National Railways—in the days of the big race to span a continent built their lines so close together over the low Yellowhead Pass that at some places rival engineers could almost shake hands with each other. Today that same pass is again in

Alberta's future as the place to span with a pipeline to carry the Province's oil to the west coast.

It was in 1922 that Jasper hit the tourist guides with a bang. That was the year the railway's big enterprise, Jasper Park Lodge, was first projected on the world's travel screens. Between the coming of the railway and 1922, Fred and Jack Brewster, mountain transportation people whose names are as familiar in the Rockies as the peaks themselves, had operated Jasper Park Camp, known to the élite as Lac Beauvert and to those who could not pronounce Beauvert as the Tent City.

Jasper Park Lodge, the cottage and cabin hotel, today occupies the site on the shores of Lac Beauvert with Mount Edith Cavell on one side, Pyramid Mountain on the other, bears running all over the golf links where Bing Crosby in 1947 won the famous Totem Pole Tournament, and waiters riding bicycles hither and yon, steering with one hand and balancing trays with the other.

For such a big and so popular enterprise, Jasper Park Lodge actually had a quaint beginning. The main lodge and cabin lodges trace some of their architecture to a cabin occupied years ago by an old squatter named Swift. The man who dreamed the design, John Schofield, decided the Athabaska Valley was no place for a massive hotel, and how right he was. The first draft design for the first building was made in one afternoon in 1920 by a young English chap, George Milnes, who only a few hours before had wandered into C.N.R. offices in Montreal looking for a job.

Jackpine for the first bungalows came from the site, and so did the stones. The cabins, snuggled amid the trees today, range from four to twenty-three rooms and the main building is reputed to be the largest single storey log structure in the world. To lay out the famous and fabulous golf course, which was opened in 1925 by Earl Haig, commander-in-chief of the British forces in the First Great War, trainloads of soil were imported.

For the visitor with a desire to stir himself amid such luxury, Jasper offers everything from glacier skiing of the

Tonquin Valley to Miette Hot Springs with a temperature of 126 degrees. There is also the beautiful Maligne Lake and Mount Edith Cavell, and about seventy miles south on the way to that other fabulous place, Banff, there are the Columbia Ice Fields, 150 square miles in extent. From a chalet in the valley, snowmobiles take thousands each year three miles up the ice to get a good idea of what the rest of it is like. From the summit of Mount Snow Dome (11,340 feet) to the Athabaska Glacier, is one of the longest glacial descents in the world, a drop of 5,000 feet in seven miles. The whole area is a weird and chilly place with ice sprawling like a huge frozen hand.

As you move southward in this land of great but also frightening beauty you pass places with such picturesque names as Valley of the Crooked Trees, Honeymoon Lake, Sunwapta Falls, Beauty Creek and Tangle Creek and Red-earth Creek and The Graveyard (where gravel flats are littered with whitened driftwood resembling bones) and everywhere around you are mountains.

This 150-mile strip of gravel—the Banff-Jasper road—that today is a road of good times for thousands every summer, was built as a road of hard times. Projected in 1931 as a relief measure and completed in 1941, it produced during its construction one oddity. Or maybe it was three. Three queer holes were found about fourteen miles north of Saskatchewan Crossing. Covered by moss and vegetation, they were located when a horse stepped into one of them. One hole was about twenty inches in diameter, the other two about eighteen inches each, and each hole went down vertically for about twenty feet.

There had been no drilling or anything of that nature in the area. There was no road there until these relief labourers came along with their horses and wheelbarrows. And C. M. Walker, the man who was in charge of surveying and engineering and to whose attention the holes were drawn, thought they may have been left by trees that had rotted and the fibre turned to dust.

Walker decided that he had come to the wrong conclusion after he made some fish-hook affairs, attached them to a long pole and dropped them down the holes—to bring them up with no sign of vegetation attached thereto. So he gave up worrying about it and got on with the job. The holes were right in the centre of the surveyed road and they were filled in, so when passing there is no need for you to worry about them, either.

Mr. Walker is one of those men who is a mountaineer by adoption. As a young surveyor for the Canadian government he went to Banff in 1912 to re-survey the townsite—the original survey was in 1885 and covered enough territory to build a city—and when he retired in 1948 he still called Banff home.

As the supervising engineer in western parks, it was Mr. Walker who planned construction of most of the park roads of today. And he can tell some good stories about them. The first roads radiated from Banff which in itself was rather peculiar because apart from a trail from Calgary there was no way for anybody with a car to get to Banff. The Canadian government in its wisdom of the day apparently figured most of the tourists would come from the United States and the road to Windermere was partially finished before any decent road was built to Calgary. It was in 1913 that the British Columbia government started portions of the present Banff-Windermere highway and the Canadian government the section from the B.C. boundary to the junction of the present Banff-Lake Louise road at Castle Mountain, now Mount Eisenhower.

When Mr. Walker was instructed that same year to locate the Banff-Lake Louise road it was with the stipulation that he should see what could be done to keep it within a cost of $4,000 per mile and for a speed limit of 20 miles an hour. Today that 40 miles of black-top is just an hour's drive but for the surveying crew an advance of a quarter of a mile was a good day's work.

The building of this road was started in 1914 but almost immediately hit by the outbreak of war. At Massive, about fourteen miles west of Banff, the government set up a camp for enemy aliens and to keep them out of mischief gave them wheelbarrows, picks and shovels and put them to work to build a scenic road now known throughout the continent. The road was completed in 1920, black-topped by 1941 after another war had interfered with its destiny.

It is at Lake Louise Junction, thirty-six miles west of Banff, that you strike this main artery upon coming down the Jasper road, but before that for some miles you have been travelling in Banff National Park which, just as its scenery differs from Jasper, has a history of its own.

One of the first white men on record to see what is now Banff was Rev. Robert T. Rundle, a missionary who wandered into its beauties in 1840 and after whom a mountain at Banff is named. Its start as a national park goes back to 1885, and, the story goes, is the result of a dispute between a couple of railway surveyors who had staked spots for themselves at some hot springs on Sulphur Mountain. The surveyors had some dispute as to who owned what and it was referred to a government tribunal which decided with commendable wisdom that the whole area was such a beautiful place it should belong to the people of Canada. Ten square miles set aside around the hot springs as a result became the start of Canada's first national park that is today one of the world's most famous.

For the visitors to Banff today the chair lift up Mount Norquay, the castle-like Banff Springs Hotel and its golf course, Lake Minnewanka and its boat trip, the Cave and Basin and the Sulphur Springs, where signs in winter ask people not to throw snowballs in the pool, are among its fabulous attractions. And only forty miles to the west it has for a neighbour beautiful Lake Louise that reflects white Victoria Glacier from one side and the charming white chateau from the other, a place that the late Ernie Pyle, the roving American newspaperman, described as one of the most beautiful in the world.

These two beautiful and tremendous hotel buildings, the Banff Springs Hotel and Chateau Lake Louise, trace their origin to the mind of Sir William Van Horne when he was president of the Canadian Pacific Railway. Van Horne is on record as saying that "since we cannot export the scenery we shall have to import the tourists." But the first mountain hotels operated by the railway were not tourist hotels at all. They were places for the passengers to eat. The grades were so steep that the operation of dining cars on the trains was not feasible, so the passengers, as far back as 1886 and for some years after, hopped off at Field, Glacier, Revelstoke and North Bend to dine in a railway-operated hotel.

The Banff Springs Hotel, a summer retreat for thousands of vacationists each year, and for as many more a place to wander around and admire, was started in 1887. The design was by a leading American architect, Bruce Price, and Van Horne specified it should be of the French chateau type of architecture in tribute to the French explorers whose path the C.P.R. followed.

The first big function held in the hotel was a ball in 1898 attended by the governor-general, Lord Stanley, accompanied by Frederick Villiers, of the *Illustrated London News,* and regardless of what the *London News* said of it, the affair was the talk of Canada. The hotel did not always look as it looks today. It was added to, bit by bit, in 1911, 1914, and between 1926 and 1928 it was practically rebuilt. It was much the same with the Chateau Lake Louise. It was built in 1890. It was a wooden structure up to 1926 when that burned down and the present building was erected. Just whose idea it was to plant the Icelandic poppies along the lakeshore and lawn flower beds has been lost in the years, but there is some suggestion that that too was Van Horne's idea.

Those are among the things for a man to see at Banff and Lake Louise today, but for the fellow who likes a spot of history there are other things, too, although he should know full well they will be largely in his mind's eye. Among the remnants of yesteryear there are Silver City and Bankhead, the former once the home of 3,000 persons seeking silver and the latter of 1,700 who mined coal and whose backyard was the scene of probably the first movie thriller ever filmed in Canada.

What was Silver City is today just a stretch of flat, grassy land at the foot of Mount Eisenhower, that beautiful castle-like mountain once known as Castle Mountain but renamed in tribute to the American General Ike Eisenhower, much to the consternation of mountain men. They were all in favour of paying tribute to Eisenhower but by picking some other mountain to bear his name, not by changing the name of one that was so aptly named in the first place that school children would say at first glance that it looked like a castle.

There is nothing left of Silver City, of course. At least nothing that you would expect of a ghost town. No wind-worried cabins with doors leaning on creaking hinges. No fences hidden by weeds. No grizzled old prospector, as gnarled as the trees, living in the quiet recesses of his mind. Nothing like that. There is life and plenty of it, but it whizzes by on the Banff-Lake Louise highway. It does not remember Silver City and there is nothing there to cause it to pause and ponder. On one side of the flat there is a camp for entomologists. On the other side of the flat there is the main line of the C.P.R., a section man's home and a shack that serves as a station and on which is a sign to say Winnipeg is 938 miles in one direction and Vancouver is 543 miles in the other. But nowhere, except what may be in the mind's eye, is there anything to say that here the twain once met.

Inside the station there is a long, flat and shining black stove to keep warm whoever may seek shelter after putting out the green and white flags by day or the green and white lanterns that stop the train by night. In the backyard there are deer and in the trees there are birds. And all around are the stone-faced neighbours that once fathered Silver City.

In 1881 word got around that there was silver thereabouts. Two years or so later the railway brought the rich-hungry by the thousands. A place of 3,000 souls, then larger than Fort Calgary, sprang up. People chipped and hacked into the mountains all around. Today there is what you could dignify as the remnants of a mine a mile and a half from the flats.

The silver fever was not of long duration and it was not fatal. But it built a real city before its disillusioned people began to drift elsewhere, leaving their buildings to be torn down and nothing left but Joe Smith.

Joe Smith was from Quebec and he got out west with railway construction. For some reason he stayed at Silver City after the others left. He was eighty-two and almost blind in 1937 when well-meaning friends took him to a home. But his spirit remained in his old cabin and in Silver City and a month after they moved him, he joined it. And with him died the last link with Silver City.

It was not quite so sad at Bankhead. There are still people around who mined or worked there. People like D. M. Soole, who was the town's postmaster from 1907 to 1913 and who lately has been in the real estate business in Banff, where he was one of the community's first Mounties. In those days, around 1904, the town's Mounties got fifty cents a day for reading water meters, and shared in such costs as the fifty cents people paid to retrieve horses and cows from the pound, and with what they collected in court costs from imbibing citizens, it was a pretty fair paying proposition.

Bankhead is one of two old industrial sites near Banff. The other is Anthracite. Lot titles for Anthracite go back to 1887 and it is now the only free-hold property in the park although subservient to park regulations. What was Anthracite is today just a pile of coal at the junction of the main highway and the road to Lake Minnewanka, but when the Anthracite Coal Company closed in 1904 there were company buildings, a store and thirty dwellings there.

Bankhead, about five miles along the Lake Minnewanka road that branches out from Banff past the garbage grounds where the tourists go to watch well-fed bears of an evening, is also a ghost although it has a little more to show for its efforts.

The Canadian Pacific Railway opened Bankhead about 1905 and the story is that about $7,000,000 was poured into the place to get out hard coal before it fell before competition of Drumheller, which had coal that was softer but easier to get. Even after that blow the company kept fighting for fifteen years to keep the place going by manufacturing the first briquettes made in Canada, using pitch that was imported from Kentucky. In its hey-day the place had 1,700 residents and they enjoyed water and sewer long before it got to Banff. It had other refinements, too, including fourteen establishments known as "blind pigs" and when they proved too much for everybody the place acquired a hotel. Tunnels that were twenty feet wide burrowed into the mountain and the coal came out in little cars that also provided the thrills for probably the first movie made in Canada.

The film company came from New York. The year was 1909. The excited heroine the company brought along came a-yelling on one of the coal cars from out of the mine. The hero galloped past Soole's post office and snatched the fair miss from certain death as clean as a whistle. People who can recall the affair, say the coal cars were not moving half as fast as the guy on horseback.

There are a few odds and ends of Bankhead left. The concrete steps on the knoll within view of the highway are what remains of the Catholic church. When Bankhead died it was cut in half, moved on flat cars to Calgary and today is in that city's Forest Lawn suburb. There are still the foundations of what were the tipple, briquetting plant and even basements of substantial homes that were long since moved to Banff.

On the highway where the milestone indicates that Banff is exactly five miles away, there is a war memorial. Banff veterans come each year after their own Remembrance Day service to honour old Bankhead warriors whose names are carved on the picturesque monument that is set in the pines, a Union Jack flying behind it.

It is a far cry from the days when the place had a payroll of $45,000, a few greenbacks that once got lost. The money used to be shipped from Calgary and Soole would pick it up at the Bankhead station. The train, however, did not stop. The mail clerk kicked the bags out in general direction of the depot. One night in a blizzard he didn't know just where he was, but took a chance anyway. When Soole came to the depot with his team the bags were nowhere in sight. Soole got the station agent and section men for miles around to help search. The sun was up and the mountains well aired before they found them buried in a snowdrift some distance up the track. After that the money was sent with an escort.

Few of the thousands of summer visitors ever realize that Banff is more than a summer resort. For some 2,500 people it is a year-round home and they are seeing it rapidly developing into a winter resort, too, where you can either ski down the mountain slopes or swim in the outdoor sulphur pool. Most of the permanent residents make their living from the tourist traffic, either by directing it in one form or another or by selling it something ranging from accommodation to souvenirs. Some of the residents fashion the souvenirs in the winter months, but many of them come stamped "Made in Ontario."

To these people, the mountains are part of their lives and they cannot understand why some visitors complain of feeling "hemmed in." Ralph Edwards, down at the government information bureau, always contends he dislikes the prairie country because it frightens him. He says you can get lost on the prairies but it is impossible to get lost in the mountains, because you are always in a valley so the logical thing to do, if somewhat bewildered, is to turn around and return from where you came.

In his day Edwards has climbed many mountains and trailed through many mountain valleys. He likes to recall the days when a trip to Lake Louise from Banff took a day and a half by pack train and a jaunt to Jasper took two weeks. Edwards came from England in 1895 when he was seventeen. He intended to farm, but two weeks of that life at Lachine, Quebec, settled those notions so he moved to Banff and has not been east of Calgary since, and it is not very often that he bothers to go to Calgary.

For years Edwards worked with the pack train outfits in the days when the tourists were more interested in a rugged vacation and not so keen about doing their mountain climbing the easy way as they do today by reaching the 7,000 foot level on Mount Norquay by riding the chair lift that rises a vertical distance of 1,300 feet in ten minutes.

Edwards' eyes are bright behind the shadows of his beetle brows and they appear puzzled when visitors tell him the mountains are always the same. As Edwards well knows, the play of the light makes them change by the hour. And they have given Edwards three firsts. In the days when a top guide made $50 a month and grub from July to October, and about as much on the side, Edwards was with the first party to see the Yoho Valley, with the first pack train over Dolomite Pass, and with the first party to ascend Mount Balfour.

In 1897 he was with a party hired by Prof. J. Harbel, of the University of Strasbourg, with the intention of climbing Mount Balfour. They thought they would tackle it from the west side, and in getting around to it became the first to see what was ultimately named the Yoho Valley. The following year Edwards went up Balfour from the Bow side with another party.

It is funny the attractions the mountains have for people. And how they hold them. You take Charlie Beil. He is no mountain man. He was a ranch hand, originally. But in the quiet of Banff's mountains he has made a continental name for himself as a sculptor. Beil was sitting in his studio, comfortable-like on a stool much as a man would sit on a horse with one leg over the saddle horn, and as he told me about how all this had happened to him he laughed over the days when he raffled all the jackasses. In those days he was on the pay-roll of various ranchers down in the American range country as a wrangler. With his buddies he drifted around a lot in those days and when the grubstake got low between bunk houses, he would mould another jackass and raffle it in the gambling halls of any nearby town. He found that by kneading clay he could finance what he needed until he could tie up with the next outfit that needed a man to look after the horses. He saw a lot of country from horseback and it was what he saw from a horse that caused him to drop rein in Banff about 1930. He had been working in Nevada and to get to Montana decided to take the long way through the eastern United States then across Canada. When he got to Banff he hired a horse and rode all over the place and was so taken with it that he never did get to Montana.

It was a Montanan who really blazed the trail of Beil's future. In 1921 Beil was a guide at Glacier National Park and he met the late Charlie Russell, famous painter of cowboy and western scenes. Russell influenced Beil to look upon sculpture as a livelihood and not as a hobby. Beil spent nine years in Montana, most of it in Russell's company, but each winter he would go to California to study. As his reputation grew he was commissioned to do work for Will Rogers and William S. Hart. Some of his work today is in the Will Rogers Museum. Another piece, his "Range Rider," was presented by the Calgary Kiwanis Club to Viscount Bennett and in turn willed by Viscount Bennett to the Society for Promotion of Arts in London.

Beil first makes his models in clay, then casts them in plaster of Paris, then a wax cast and then in bronze. When a model is finished you can hit it with a hammer and it will ring like a bell. He does all his own research, depending upon memory, observation, sketches and photographs. And he wishes today that somebody would do something about unearthing some old wagon wheels. Real wagon wheels. The kind they wrote songs about. He figures they are going the way of the jerk-line team, which is something else he wants to capture in bronze. A jerk team was a hitch of eighteen or twenty horses or mules, driven by line from the lead horse or mule. And in wanting to preserve this sight in bronze, Beil actually reveals the true purpose of his life as he lives it today in Alberta's mountains. He has dedicated his skill to preserving a yesteryear. He feels people forget their roots too soon.

The mountains are full of creative people. They spend their lives quietly, painting, sketching, writing or following the more modern art of photography. So Banff, then, is really more than a playground. It is also a studio and because of the Banff School of Fine Arts it is also a classroom.

To talk with the director of this school, Donald Cameron, is a revelation because he associates art with hunger and not with long hair. It is that hunger for knowledge that he believes will eventually see the Banff School of Fine Arts a Canadian Salzburg. It may take fifteen years, but they are working on it.

Cameron himself is a bit of a revelation. This man who directs the extension department of the University of Alberta, which also directs the school, is a son of the soil. His father, also named Donald, was an Innisfail, Alberta, homesteader and a farmer party member of the Alberta legislature from 1921 to 1935. It was the old-time meetings of neighbour farmers in the Cameron home that got young Donald Cameron interested in farm organization work. He studied at the University of Alberta on a department of agriculture scholarship, but while studying for his master's degree in agriculture economics he saw the possibilities of adult education.

So in 1930 he entered the education field with an appointment to the university's extension service. In 1933 he studied adult education in Europe on a Carnegie scholarship. Three years later he was named director of the extension service and also the Banff school, which meant he acquired two comfortable homes, one in Edmonton for the winter and one at Banff for the summer.

The Banff School of Fine Arts today draws students from most of Canada, the United States, Norway, Hawaii, Mexico and Alaska, to name a few places, but it had a poor cousin beginning. It was started in 1933 on a Carnegie grant to the University of Alberta to encourage fine arts. The authorities thought about forty people would turn up, but one hundred and thirty responded to the opportunity to study stage production and acting in the old Dr. Brett theatre at the sanitorium. When they had a full house Cameron spent most of his time running downstairs to make sure the beams were holding.

These summers the school draws up to six hundred pupils to what is now a major continuation centre of the university.

The school owns three beautiful chalets on a site second in Banff only to that occupied by the Banff Springs Hotel. It owns ten cabins and can in its own right accommodate three hundred for sleeping. Its summer sessions are the highlight of the calendar, of course, but the school now offers up to twenty-eight short courses during the year and what with other gatherings it operates nine months of the year and draws some three thousand persons to Banff. Of a summer day you see some of them sitting by the roadside painting or sketching; doing a nimble ballet on some grassy knoll or vocalizing in some quiet nook in the valley.

The school's future is on the drawing boards. In Mr. Cameron's office there is an artist's conception of the Canadian Salzburg to come. Much of this depends upon the success of the Banff Foundation, a plan to enlist Canadian citizens on a nation-wide basis to create a Canadian art centre in a setting only Canada can provide. When the school has its own accommodation for 1,000, it can operate on a year-round basis. But the plans are for the material things. The policy was set, or maybe it just grew, as the school advanced from drama to arts, music, playwriting and painting. No matter what the growth of the school, the policy will remain the same: to invite as guest instructors leading artists of the world to develop a richer Canadian culture in the friendly atmosphere of the Canadian west. And the man who at the moment is doing the inviting is a one-time Alberta farm boy who got his education in a one-room country school.

Men of the mountains made a stab years ago at developing the arts. As you leave Banff, following the black-top the eighty-seven miles eastward to Calgary—and negotiating the Exshaw hill which, back in 1913 when cars became popular, motorists climbed in reverse because the gas tank was under the front seat and that was the only way they could keep the gas flowing—you come to a mining town known as Canmore. Canmore is a little different, perhaps, than most mining communities because of its beautiful setting. It is here you can find a story of pioneering in Canadian art, for in Canmore's little United Church, Dr. C. W. Gordon penned his first historical novels under the name of Ralph Connor. And a few blocks up the street there is a log cabin theatre where travelling British opera companies trod the boards years ago.

At the church you may meet Rev. Robert H. MacKinnon, D.D., a stoutish, good-natured fellow who would take you through the building with the air of a man who quite regularly goes through a sight-seeing routine. Dr. MacKinnon deems it an honour to be the minister of the little frame church that was built in 1890 when the minister of the day, Dr. Gordon, would do his writing in the lamplight of a back room. Canmore and its people were the background and Dr. Gordon's enlarged study is today known as Gordon Memorial Hall, a social centre for the congregation.

On the lawn there is a cairn erected by the United Church in 1942 to honour Dr. Gordon, but it is a name that lives much farther afield. Dr. MacKinnon has found it is known to practically all Canadians and to most Americans who visit the church, and in the course of each summer visitors number around three hundred, all induced to leave the main highway and drive into town by a modest sign, "visit Canmore's historic church."

The church stands also as a symbol of the love and respect that is embodied in the meaning of the words family and neighbour to the people of this mountain community. The church stands in the shadows of the Three Sisters, on a winding street lined with frame homes of mining people. The windows, doors, even tables have been dedicated by various members of the congregation to their loved ones, some killed in the wars, some in mine or other tragedies.

In a little log cabin up the street, a quaint building protected by the rugged and towering Chinaman's Peak against the slip stream of the years that has whistled through Whitman's Pass, there are memories of another kind.

They call it the Opera House and it has been that, but also a place for dancing and a place where the miners' band practiced and the minstrels played. But like an old gentleman with gnarled features it has retained its dignity in face of opposition from a more modern theatre in the town.

Canmore people believe it is the only theatre of its kind in Canada. Some contend it is the only one of its kind on the continent. If you stay around long enough, you will be sure to meet somebody who will claim there has never been anything like it anywhere. It has been standing since 1898 and its very appearance today could help a dreamer escape reality, until he becomes acquainted with the candy machine in the tiny lobby and the exposed pipes that run along the wall to carry steam heat, and if you have been in a log cabin that is steam heated you have been in a place that is really warm.

The old Opera House remembers when the miners danced the polka and the squares to scrapings of the local orchestra. It remembers the minstrel show days and the travelling operas. In 1932 it saw the change of the screen talking and the audience keeping quiet and to help the acoustics the walls were lined with beaverboard.

The miners snaked the sturdy pine logs from the forest to build what at first was a structure forty feet long and twenty-six feet wide. In 1926 the International Welsh Choir somehow got its cast of twenty-four on the stage that is sixteen feet deep with a twenty foot opening. Once, too, the British National Opera Company stopped over to play "The Bohemian Girl." As William Ramsay, who retired a while ago from his job as timekeeper at the mine, put it, those were the two happiest mistakes he had made while running the theatre. He enjoyed the performances but neither paid.

The theatre is not advertised as an attraction of Canmore in any way, but word of its presence seems to trickle around the mountains and leaders of the entertainment world visiting Banff always ask to be taken to see it. Mr. Ramsay said hundreds of snapshots have been taken of it, and he has often wondered just how Ginger Rogers made out the dull day she photographed it from all angles.

And so on eastward. Over the Exshaw hill that used to give so much trouble—those were the days when motorists had to get out of the park before dark because use of headlights was prohibited; somebody thought it would frighten the animals—and past the Canada Cement Company's plant in the shadow of a great mountain of limestone that provides the basic materials, and will continue to do so for centuries. A regular old man of a mountain.

On past the home of the Stoneys, the Morley Indian reservation, past the wind-beaten old church that served the people for so many years, sitting lonely and quiet in a field far back from the cairn marking the historical site that commemorates the coming of the missionaries—in the country where one of them, Rev. George McDougall was frozen in 1874. Then along the beautiful Bow and then up the Cochrane Hill with its Lookout Point that presents all the beauties of the mountains and the foothills in one wide sweep.

And so on to Calgary, the cowtown which has all of this in its very backyard to make it the most fortunate city in Canada's most fortunate Province.

INDEX

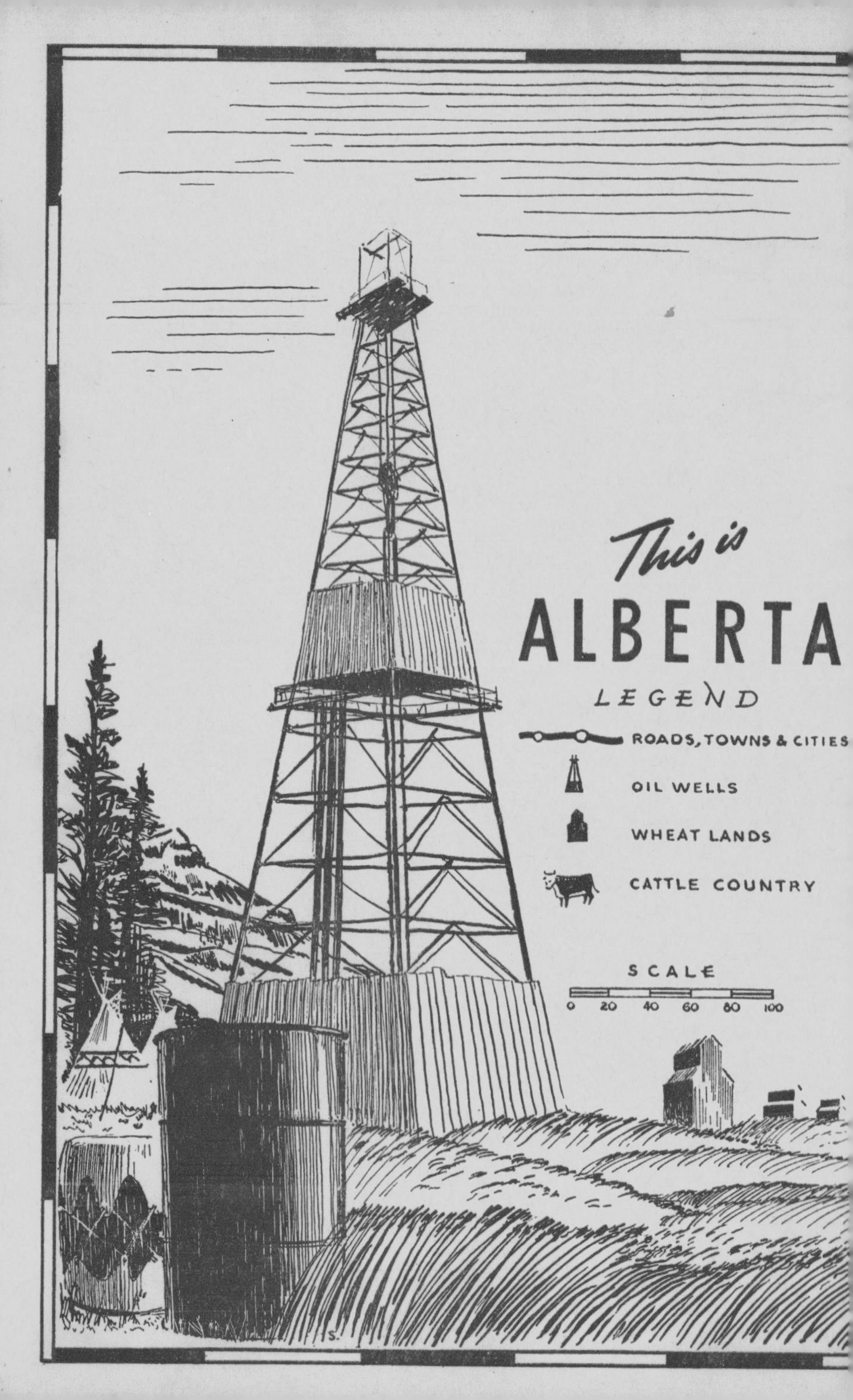
This is
ALBERTA
LEGEND
ROADS, TOWNS & CITIES
OIL WELLS
WHEAT LANDS
CATTLE COUNTRY
SCALE
0 20 40 60 80 100
S.